The Soapy Murder Case

A Farce in Three Acts

by Tim Kelly

Single copies of plays are sold for reading purposes only. The copying or duplicating of a play, or any part of play, by hand or by any other process, is an infringement of the copyright. Such infringement will be vigorously prosecuted.

**Baker's Plays
7611 Sunset Blvd.
Los Angeles, CA 90042
bakersplays.com**

NOTICE

This book is offered for sale at the price quoted only on the understanding that, if any additional copies of the whole or any part are necessary for its production, such additional copies will be purchased. The attention of all purchasers is directed to the following: this work is fully protected under the copyright laws of the United States of America, the British Commonwealth, including Canada, and all other countries of the Copyright Union. Violations of the Copyright Law are punishable by fine or imprisonment, or both. The copying or duplication of this work or any part of this work, by hand or by any process, is an infringement of the copyright and will be vigorously prosecuted.

This play may not be produced by amateurs or professionals for public or private performance without first submitting application for performing rights. Royalties are due on all performances whether for charity or gain, or whether admission is charged or not. Since performance of this play without the payment of the royalty fee renders anybody participating liable to severe penalties imposed by the law, anybody acting in this play should be sure, before doing so, that the royalty fee has been paid. Professional rights, reading rights, radio broadcasting, television and all mechanical rights, etc. are strictly reserved. Application for performing rights should be made directly to BAKER'S PLAYS.

No one shall commit or authorize any act or omission by which the copyright of, or the right to copyright, this play may be impaired. No one shall make any changes in this play for the purpose of production.

Publication of this play does not imply availability for performance. Both amateurs and professionals considering a production are strongly advised in their own interest to apply to Baker's Plays for written permission before starting rehearsals, advertising, or booking a theatre.

Whenever the play is produced, the author's name must be carried in all publicity, advertising and programs. Also, the following notice must appear on all printed programs, "Produced by special arrangement with Baker's Plays."

Licensing fees for *THE SOAPY MURDER CASE* is based on a per performance rate and payable one week in advance of the production.

Please consult the Baker's Plays website at www.bakersplays.com or our current print catalogue for up to date licensing fee information.

Copyright © 1979 by Tim Kelly
Made in U.S.A.
All rights reserved.

THE SOAPY MURDER CASE
ISBN **978-0-87440-591-0**
#21246-B

CHARACTERS

(In Order of Appearance)

HORATIO TUCKER, *a crotchety recluse, business tycoon and multi-millionaire.*

MRS. NAUGAHIDE, *his housekeeper.*

IVY M. ROBESPIERRE, *a television executive, cold, efficient, a person you love to hate.*

LINK KENNECOTT, *television director, young and outgoing.*

DOTTIE DUNCAN, *pretty young actress, not too bright, harbors a strange secret.*

JESSICA COURTNEY, *a glamorous actress who lives in fear of Ivy.*

DR. BROCK RITTENHOUSE, *a television actor who lives his part day and night.*

DAVID SOMERSET, *an actor with a cop's personality.*

MONA LA MOOCH, *a "saintly mother" actress.*

PHIL REINHOLT, *a "Joe College" type.*

SYNOPSIS

PLACE: *The penthouse apartment of Horatio Tucker, New York City.*

TIME: *The Present.*

ACT ONE

The living room, a summer evening.

ACT TWO

The same. Later.

ACT THREE

The same. Still later.

The Soapy Murder Case

ACT ONE

SETTING: *The living room in the penthouse apartment of* HORATIO TUCKER, *a crotchety recluse, business tycoon and multi-millionaire.* APPROXIMATELY DOWN RIGHT CENTER *is a table with two matching chairs.* UP RIGHT *there is a narrow table, buffet or sideboard—another* UP LEFT. *On each can be found handsomely-bound books, expensive bric-a-brac, decanters and glasses, etc. On the* UP RIGHT *table is a bowl of apples. Between these tables,* UP CENTER, *is a rather large fireplace with a mantel above that features a framed award or plaque, given to a television program that* HORATIO *has sponsored for several seasons—*"THE BEST TEARS OF OUR LIVES." DOWN CENTER *there is a comfortable sofa angled, somewhat, from the fireplace.* APPROXIMATELY DOWN LEFT *there is a large armchair with a sidetable to the* LEFT. *Entrance into the apartment is* LEFT. *We can catch a glimpse of an entry hallway. Off this hallway, unseen, is the library.* EXIT *into other areas of the penthouse is* RIGHT, *which leads into another hallway; a table and floral arrangement can be seen in this hallway. On each side of this* EXIT *can be found a chair. Above the chair* UPSTAGE *of* EXIT *is a portrait of* HORATIO TUCKER *as a young man—a dour, sour, pickle of a man. A small panel for some light switches is by the portrait. To these basic properties should be added various items that will "dress up" the stage—carpets, lamps, wall sconces, pictures and the like. Despite the fact the room reflects wealth, there is a certain studied "effect" about it as if the room were the set for a television soap opera.*

THE SOAPY MURDER CASE — ACT I

AT RISE: HORATIO TUCKER, *president of "Tucker's Tasty Pudding Powder and All-Purpose Detergent" sits in the armchair bundled up in a blanket, a shawl over his shoulders. He's ill-tempered, unpleasant, dictatorial and spiteful. He has weak eyes, bushy eyebrows, wears spectacles. There's a tray with medicine bottles on the table to his* LEFT. HORATIO *sneezes, again, and, then—again.*

HORATIO. MRS. NAUGAHIDE! (*Another sneeze. He takes a handkerchief from his pocket and blows his nose —loudly*) MRS. NAUGAHIDE! Where are you, you misguided Florence Nightingale! Can't you hear me? I'm in pain. (*Mumbling, he searches through the medicine bottles at his side*) Never around when she's needed. Pay a good salary and what do I get for my money? Precious little. No wonder the country's going to the hounds. (*Picks up bottle of nose drops, studies label*) "SNIFFO —SAY GOODBYE TO NASAL DRIP." (*Takes out stopper*) I'd fire the agency that came up with that slogan. (*Tilts his head back, pushes spectacles to his forehead, prepares to use the nose drops*) MRS. NAUGAHIDE! (*He squeezes a drop as* MRS. NAUGAHIDE ENTERS RIGHT. *She wears a dark dress*)

MRS. NAUGAHIDE. What's all the shouting about, Mr. Tucker?

HORATIO. (*As nose drop hits*) O-o-o-o-o-w!

MRS. NAUGAHIDE. Good gracious, what is it!

HORATIO. The nose drop went into my eye. (MRS. NAUGAHIDE *crosses to the armchair. She's a pleasant lady who doesn't seem to be intimidated by her demanding employer. However, whenever she discusses the plots of television soap operas she rambles on, sounding like the text in the worst of fan magazines. She takes the bottle and returns it to the tray*)

MRS. NAUGAHIDE. Why are you using nose drops?

HORATIO. I use what I choose to use. (*Wipes at eyes, adjusts spectacles*)

MRS. NAUGAHIDE. You don't have a cold.

HORATIO. Didn't you hear me sneezing?

ACT I THE SOAPY MURDER CASE 7

Mrs. Naugahide. You told me you had an allergy. You didn't say anything about a cold.

Horatio. Cold, allergy—what's the difference when I'm in discomfort?

Mrs. Naugahide. (*Picks up some bottle*) Have you taken your Magnetic Liver Pills?

Horatio. No, and I'm not going to. They make the fillings in my teeth tingle.

Mrs. Naugahide. (*Returns bottle to tray, picks up another*) It's time for your anti-acid neutralizer.

Horatio. Bah!

Mrs. Naugahide. (*Returns bottle, picks up another, studies it*) You haven't touched your peppery Nerve Tonic.

Horatio. You drink it. I can't abide the stuff.

Mrs. Naugahide. (*Picks up a tablespoon, prepares to pour some nerve tonic*) Open your mouth.

Horatio. I won't drink it, I tell you.

Mrs. Naugahide. You said the doctor said—

Horatio. The doctor's a quack. All doctors are quacks. (Mrs. Naugahide *manages to get a spoonful of tonic into his mouth while he's complaining. He's caught unaware, makes a frightening face*)

Mrs. Naugahide. (*Like a mother chiding a naughty child*) Don't you spit that out, Mr. Tucker. Swallow it.

Horatio. (*Enraged, clinches his hands; he really wants to spit it out, but forces himself to swallow*) Ugh! What do they make that nerve tonic from! Tastes like an old shoe.

Mrs. Naugahide. I wouldn't know, Mr. Tucker. I've never tasted an old shoe.

Horatio. (*Impatient*) Take away this tray, get it out of my sight. If old age doesn't get me, my medicine will. (*Sharply*) Take it away, I said.

Mrs. Naugahide. (*Picks up the tray of medicine bottles*, Crosses *to* Up Left *table and puts it down*) You're excited this evening. Won't do your blood pressure any good.

Horatio. Worry about your own blood pressure. Did you call down to the desk?

Mrs. Naugahide. I told the doorman you were expecting several guests this evening and not to buzz the penthouse. He said he'd send them right up.

HORATIO. Good. Can't abide that buzzer. *Buzz-buzz-buzz.* When it sounds I get the feeling I'm being attacked by a swarm of killer bees.

MRS. NAUGAHIDE. (*Moving* RIGHT *of* HORATIO) It's for your own security, Mr. Tucker. One never knows who's prowling about.

HORATIO. I know who's prowling about. It's *you.* Never know what you're up to half the time.

MRS. NAUGAHIDE. Would you care for some warm nonfat milk? (HORATIO *sticks his tongue out like a brat, makes a distasteful sound*) We are in a mood to be difficult this evening.

HORATIO. Mind your tongue and fetch me my cane. I want my wheelchair, too.

MRS. NAUGAHIDE. You should use your walker, Mr. Tucker. You need the exercise. (DOORBELL) What's that?

HORATIO. (*Snide*) Do you suppose it could be the doorbell?

MRS. NAUGAHIDE. I believe you're right.

HORATIO. Are you going to stand there and discuss the possibility, or are you going to answer it!

MRS. NAUGAHIDE. I'll answer it, of course.

HORATIO. Go along, go along. (MRS. NAUGAHIDE *Exits* LEFT. HORATIO *roars out—*) *But first fetch me my cane!* (MRS. NAUGAHIDE *returns immediately, a walking stick or cane she's taken from somewhere in the hallway in her grip. She* CROSSES *to* HORATIO *and holds it out*)

MRS. NAUGAHIDE. Your cane, Mr. Tucker. (*He grabs it from her, angrily.* DOORBELL) There it is again.

HORATIO. It's a comfort to know you're not going deaf. Would it be too much if I suggested you show in my first guest?

MRS. NAUGAHIDE. (EXITING LEFT) That's what you pay me for.

HORATIO. (*Grumbles*) A waste of good money. Why do I keep her on? Insubordinate female. (*He tosses aside the blanket and, with the aid of his cane, stands. He's none-too-steady and makes all kinds of wheezes and grunts*)

ACT I THE SOAPY MURDER CASE 9

MRS. NAUGAHIDE'S VOICE. If you'll come this way. Mr. Tucker is expecting you.
IVY'S VOICE. Thank you. (*Still mumbling and grumbling,* HORATIO *manages to hobble* CENTER)
MRS. NAUGAHIDE. (ENTERS) It's a Miss Ivy M. Robespierre.
HORATIO. (*Testy*) Well, well, where is she? I told you to get my wheelchair.
MRS. NAUGAHIDE. I can't do two things at once, Mr. Tucker, besides the walker would be better for you.
HORATIO. *The wheelchair!*
MRS. NAUGAHIDE. Yes, sir. Right away, sir. (*She* CROSSES RIGHT)
HORATIO. Put on an apron. How's anyone going to know you're a servant?
MRS. NAUGAHIDE. I'm sure you'll tell them, sir. (*She's out*)
HORATIO. (*Tugs at his shawl*) That woman's got too much mouth. (*A command*) Come in, Miss Robespierre.

(IVY M. ROBESPIERRE *appears in the entryway. She's a cold, efficient type. She carries an attaché case and is fashionably, if severely, dressed. She extends her hand as soon as she* ENTERS, CROSSES)

IVY. Ah, H.T., you have no idea what an honor this is.
HORATIO. (*Snarls*) For you or for me?
IVY. For both of us, naturally. I knew one day I would have the pleasure of encountering the legendary Horatio Tucker face to face. (*Since* HORATIO *makes no attempt to shake hands,* IVY *pretends to wipe off a piece of lint from her outfit*)
HORATIO. Did you?
IVY. We're much alike, H.T.
HORATIO. Are we?
IVY. (CROSSES *to portrait, points to it*) Young Horatio Tucker didn't make "Tucker's Tasty Pudding Powder And All-Purpose Detergent" the phenomenally successful company it is by being kind, gentle and sentimental.
HORATIO. I've never been accused of those things.
IVY. (CROSSES *to sofa, sits, attaché case pressed to her*

bosom like something precious) Nor have I. When "Tucker's Tasty Pudding Powder And All-Purpose Detergent" took on the sponsorship of television's most popular soap, I vowed that I would keep the ratings up or know the reason why. I'm not loved by the writers or the actors or the production crew, but "The Best Tears Of Our Lives" remains number one with the viewing audience.

HORATIO. (*Grudging*) How do you manage it?

IVY. (*Opens attaché case*) I have my methods. Sometimes, for example, when a certain actress is on a segment I'll notice if the ratings go up or down. If they go down and continue that way, I have the actress written out of the script.

HORATIO. Out of the script and out of a job. Excellent. (MRS. NAUGAHIDE, *wearing a starched white apron, returns,* RIGHT, *pushing a wheelchair. She bumps it into* HORATIO *with such force that he practically falls into the seat*) Watch what you're doing, you sadist!

MRS. NAUGAHIDE. There's no pleasing you, Mr. Tucker.

IVY. (*Pulls out a folder, fools with some papers*) I've checked those writers who haven't been up to snuff lately and you'll notice there are one or two actors who seem to be slipping in audience appeal. If the ratings drop, I'll chop. (*Smug laugh*) That's a little joke of mine. Chop, chop, chop. Sometimes I feel like the queen in *Alice in Wonderland*. You know—"off with his head!"

MRS. NAUGAHIDE. (*Appalled*) Good heavens!

IVY. I was speaking figuratively, Mrs., uh—

MRS. NAUGAHIDE. Naugahide. Flora Naugahide. Think of imitation leather.

HORATIO. Never mind about her. You seem to be under the impression I've summoned you here to discuss business affairs.

MRS. NAUGAHIDE. There's not much that interests Mr. Tucker outside of his aches and pains.

HORATIO. (*Irritated with her*) Applesauce! Get my blanket, get my blanket. Do you want me to freeze to death? (MRS. NAUGAHIDE CROSSES *to armchair and picks up blanket. She returns to* HORATIO *and tucks the blanket around his legs. Dialogue continues through this busi-*

ACT I   THE SOAPY MURDER CASE   11

ness) There are only two things that interest me, Miss Robespierre. The profits from "Tucker's Tasty Pudding Powder And All-Purpose Detergent" and the continuing success of the television program I sponsor.

MRS. NAUGAHIDE. (*Mounting enthusiasm*) I never miss an episode of "The Best Tears Of Our Lives." It's my favorite soap opera. I like it better than "The Romance In Helen's Tent"—that used to be my favorite. I cried real tears when Mona La Mooch, that saintly mother, thought she was going to lose her only son when he was struck down by the steam roller on his way to the American Legion hall to donate blood for the tornado victims, but thanks to the heroic efforts of Dr. Brock Rittenhouse he was able to walk and see again, even if he needs plastic surgery to restore—

HORATIO. (*Livid, cuts her off*) *Will you shut up!* (*To* Ivy) Did you ever hear such applesauce? I think the woman's going senile.

Ivy. Ah, but you see how easy it is to become addicted to the world of soaps. Mrs. Naugahide is a true fan. Bravo! (*To* MRS. NAUGAHIDE) However, I never refer to our program as a soap "opera." That has no class. I call it simply a "soap."

MRS. NAUGAHIDE. That's class?

HORATIO. Soap? Soap opera? You can call it mud for all I care. I'm not interested if the show is good, bad or indifferent. What matters is that women who watch it buy my product.

Ivy. (*All business*) We mustn't forget—women in the eighteen-to-forty age group buy seventy-five percent of all the products advertised on daytime television. (*Dives into attaché case*) I have the figures right here.

HORATIO. (*Banging his fist on the arm of the wheelchair for emphasis*) Buy "Tucker's Tasty Pudding Powder!" Buy "Tucker's Tasty Pudding Powder!" Etc.

Ivy. (*Nodding agreement, the perfect flunky, slapping her fists on the attaché case*) Buy "Tucker's Tasty Pudding Powder!" Buy "Tucker's Tasty Pudding Powder!" Etc.

MRS. NAUGAHIDE. (*Gets caught up in the spirit of the chant, marches about like a drum majorette*) Buy "Tucker's Tasty Pudding Powder!" Buy "Tucker's Tasty

Pudding Powder!" Etc. (*Both* HORATIO *and* IVY *stop chanting and look at* MRS. NAUGAHIDE *who continues on*) Buy "Tucker's Tasty Pudding Powder!" Buy "Tucker's Tasty Pudding—" (*Her voice trails off as she observes the look of absolute rage on* HORATIO'*s face. Meekly—*) Sorry. (DOORBELL) There it is again.

HORATIO. (*To* IVY) Amazing how she can detect the sound of a doorbell.

MRS. NAUGAHIDE. Shall I answer it?

HORATIO. You don't expect me to do it, do you!

MRS. NAUGAHIDE. I'll see who it is.

HORATIO. I certainly hope so. (MRS. NAUGAHIDE EXITS LEFT)

IVY. Servants *are* a problem these days. (*Another paper*) I've charted our week-to-week ratings on this sheet. (*Indicates*) Wherever the line dips it means something is wrong. Either the script, a situation the audience dislikes, or a particular performer is featured. That's when I peel my eye and keep it peeled. If the dip continues—

HORATIO. Chop, chop, chop.

IVY. Precisely.

HORATIO. You enjoy power, Miss Robespierre?

IVY. It's the only thing worth having.

MRS. NAUGAHIDE. (*Stands in the hallway*) It's a Mr. Link Kennecott and a Miss Dottie Duncan.

HORATIO. What do you think this is—a fancy dress ball, announcing everyone as they show up!

MRS. NAUGAHIDE. Only doing my job.

HORATIO. Ha!

MRS. NAUGAHIDE. (*Calls into hallway*) This way, please.

(MRS. NAUGAHIDE *steps* UP STAGE *as* LINK KENNECOTT ENTERS. *He's a good-looking young man, outgoing, over-eager, anxious to please. He* CROSSES *over to* HORATIO, *takes his hand and pumps it.* HORATIO *frowns*)

LINK. Mr. Tucker, you have no idea how delighted I was when I received your invitation to have dinner with

ACT I   THE SOAPY MURDER CASE   13

you here at your penthouse. (*He continues to shake* HORATIO's *hand vigorously*)

(DOTTIE DUNCAN *appears* LEFT. *She's a pretty young thing. Not much when it comes to brains*)

HORATIO. (*To* IVY) Who is this oaf?
IVY. Link Kennecott. (LINK *continues to pump* HORATIO's *hand*)
HORATIO. I know that, but what does he do?
IVY. He's your director.
LINK. Your head writer, too, sir.
HORATIO. *Will you stop shaking my hand! What do you think I am—a trained poodle!* I don't like to be touched.
LINK. I beg your pardon, Mr. Tucker. (*Releases grip*) I guess I'm overly excited.
DOTTIE. We all are.
HORATIO. (*Squinting*) Who's that?
DOTTIE. Dottie Duncan, Mr. Tucker.
HORATIO. Dottie Duncan Mr. Tucker? That's a strange name.
DOTTIE. (CROSSES CENTER) No, no, sir. You're running the names together. I'm Dottie Duncan. You're Mr. Tucker.
HORATIO. I know who I am, young woman. The question is—who are you?
MRS. NAUGAHIDE. She's in "The Best Tears Of Our Lives." (*To* DOTTIE) I cried real tears when you found out you were adopted and the people you thought were your real parents turned out to be reformed safecrackers.
IVY. One of our more successful episodes.
HORATIO. Duncan, you say?
DOTTIE. (*Is so flustered by* HORATIO's *gruff manner that she curtsies*) Yes, sir. Dottie Duncan—as in coffee and doughnuts.
HORATIO. Sit down, Miss Coffee. I can't abide females hovering about. Makes me think of birds of prey about to swoop down and snatch me up in their claws.

DOTTIE. I'd never do a thing like that, Mr. Tucker. Honest. Cross my heart. (*She does*)

HORATIO. (*To* LINK) She's not much with the smarts, is she? (*Sticks his thumbs to his upper teeth*) Ow!

DOTTIE. What's wrong?

HORATIO. My dentures. They're loose again. Last week when I bit into a kaiser roll it bit back.

MRS. NAUGAHIDE. I'll get your denture adhesive.

HORATIO. You'll do nothing of the kind. I'll get it myself. Knowing you, Mrs. Naugahide, you'd probably hand me a tube of airplane glue. (*He wheels his chair about,* EXITS RIGHT)

IVY. A remarkable man. Such an inspiration.

MRS. NAUGAHIDE. (*Sotto*) Can't imagine for what.

LINK. Did you say something, Mrs. Naugahide?

MRS. NAUGAHIDE. I said, make yourselves comfortable.

LINK. Thank you, Mrs. Naugapelt. We will. (*He indicates sofa and* DOTTIE *sits beside* IVY; *who moves down as if she didn't want to be too close to this recent arrival*)

MRS. NAUGAHIDE. Hide.

LINK. (*Looks about*) Why should I hide?

MRS. NAUGAHIDE. You said pelt.

LINK. Pelt?

MRS. NAUGAHIDE. Nauga*pelt*. That's not my name. My name is Mrs. Nauga*hide*. Think of imitation leather. (DOORBELL) There it is again. (*She* EXITS LEFT. LINK *moves to table* DOWN RIGHT CENTER, *sits*)

IVY. (*Haughty*) I had no idea members of the cast would be here. I thought H.T. and I would spend the evening discussing business. Alone.

DOTTIE. (*Worried*) Oh, Miss Robespierre, I hope no one is going to be written out. That's as good as death.

IVY. (*Putting papers back into her attaché case*) Mr. Tucker and I see eye to eye on that situation. Remember, when the ratings drop I chop. Nothing personal.

LINK. I think you might give people the benefit of doubt. When ratings drop they're likely to come up again.

IVY. Sometimes yes, sometimes no. I don't need you to tell me my business, Link. You stick to directing and writing. Just make certain the viewing public *likes* your

ACT I   THE SOAPY MURDER CASE   15

directing and remains *interested* in what you write. (*Hard*) We don't produce drama, Link. We produce *profits*. That's something you're inclined to forget. (*Slaps her fist against the attaché case as before*) Buy "Tucker's Tasty Pudding Powder!" Buy "Tucker's Tasty Pudding Powder!" (LINK *and* DOTTIE *exchange a guarded look*) Think of it: All those ladies buying "Tucker's Tasty Pudding Powder And All-Purpose Detergent."

DOTTIE. Do we have to?

IVY. (*Wagging an accusing finger*) Be careful of your words, Dottie. Especially when you're in the residence of the man who pays your salary.

LINK. She didn't mean anything by the comment, Miss Robespierre.

IVY. I hope not. (*Sinister*) For her sake.

DOTTIE. Gulp. (MRS. NAUGAHIDE *returns, announces*)

MRS. NAUGAHIDE. Miss Jessica Courtney and Dr. Brock Rittenhouse. (*She steps* UP STAGE)

(JESSICA *sweeps in. She's a "glamorous" creature, dressed accordingly. Very "show biz." She opens her arms to embrace* LINK)

JESSICA. Link! Link, darling! I had no idea you were going to be here. (LINK *stands, arms wide. They embrace, puckering and smacking their lips in space as if they can't find the correct locale to plant a kiss.* JESSICA *turns to the sofa,* LINK *sits*) Here's that dear, sweet child—Dottie Duncan. (*Sees* IVY) And who's this? (*Realizing who it is, her expression of gaiety fades quickly and her voice drops to a tone of barely concealed terror*) Oh, it's you, Ivy.

IVY. People address me as Ivy M. Robespierre, or Miss Robespierre—never as Ivy.

JESSICA. (*Afraid*) Yes, yes, I forgot. I hope you'll forgive me, Miss Robespierre.

LINK. Surely your mother called you Ivy.

IVY. Having parents is no excuse for familiarity.

JESSICA. (*Wanting to get as far away from* IVY *as possible flits to the table and sits beside* LINK) I've been meaning to talk to you about my dialogue, Link. It's getting a little flat.

Ivy. I'll be the judge of that.

Mrs. Naugahide. I cried real tears, Miss Courtney, when they discovered you had to have a heart operation when you were trapped in that ski lodge up in Canada and Dr. Brock didn't have any surgical instruments, so he had to operate with a tablespoon and a plastic picnic fork.

Jessica. You *are* a loyal fan.

Ivy. Mrs. Naugahide and millions like her are barometers.

Mrs. Naugahide. I don't like to think of myself as a barometer.

Ivy. Figure of speech.

Mrs. Naugahide. I like being a figure of speech even less.

(Dr. Brock Rittenhouse Enters Left. *He's dressed in hospital whites, white shoes with red socks which are quite obvious since his trousers are too short. He carries a medical bag. He's young, handsome, professional. Wears a thin moustache*)

Dr. Brock. Cozy little scene.

Link. Come in, Dr. Brock.

Dr. Brock. (*To* Mrs. Naugahide) I wonder if there is someplace I might put my medical bag? I always keep it nearby. Never know when the services of Dr. Brock Rittenhouse might be required.

Jessica. Isn't it marvelous the way Dr. Brock keeps in character. No wonder women adore him.

Dr. Brock. When I'm on the ratings are up.

Mrs. Naugahide. Let me take the bag, Dr. Brock. (*He hands her the medical bag. She* Crosses *to the* Up Right *table and puts it down.* Dr. Brock *steps behind armchair*)

Dr. Brock. I make no secret of the fact I "live" my role. Day and night, night and day. The audience trusts Dr. Brock Rittenhouse. (*Prideful*) I like it that way. (*Chest out*) Dr. Brock Rittenhouse is—solid, substantial, trustworthy.

ACT I   THE SOAPY MURDER CASE   17

JESSICA. Some people might find it unusual—you dressing and talking like a doctor all the time.

DR. BROCK. It's the secret of my portrayal. I study day and night. Night and day. If you're going to play a medical man, you ought to act like one. I'm a "method" doctor. (*Corrects himself*) I mean actor.

MRS. NAUGAHIDE. I think it's so nice you all have the same names in real life as you do in the soap.

IVY. "The Best Tears Of Our Lives" was the first soap to use the actual names of performers for the characters they portrayed.

LINK. I've always disliked that gimmick.

IVY. Fortunately, Link, I was able to overrule your objection.

LINK. I haven't forgotten.

IVY. You, Dottie Duncan, are Dottie in life and Dottie in soap. It's impossible for any member of the viewing audience to separate the real you from the fake you.

DOTTIE. Sometimes I have that problem myself.

MRS. NAUGAHIDE. (*Rubbing her side*) Dr. Brock, I've had a pain in my side for sometime. I wonder if you could tell me what it is?

DR. BROCK. I don't make house calls. (DOORBELL)

MRS. NAUGAHIDE. The bell again? More guests, I suppose. (*She* CROSSES LEFT, EXITS)

DR. BROCK. I had no idea we were all gathering.

IVY. Nor did I.

DOTTIE. Is this some special occasion?

IVY. When you receive an invitation from Horatio Tucker the occasion is special. You can be sure of that.

LINK. Must be something in the wind.

DOTTIE. (*Tentative*) Is it about our soap, Miss Robespierre?

JESSICA. (*Worried*) You're not writing anyone . . . out?

IVY. When the axe falls, Jessica, you'll be the first to know.

JESSICA. (*Alarmed*) Oh! (*She squeezes* LINK's *arm. It's obvious, that despite her sophistication, she lives in fear of* IVY *and her "chop, chop, chop"*)

LINK. I don't approve of the way you threaten people, Miss Robespierre.

IVY. (*The innocent*) Threaten? Me? What an unkind thing to say.

JESSICA. (*Impulsive*) She's going to write me out, Link. I know it.

LINK. Shhhhh. (MRS. NAUGAHIDE *returns*)

MRS. NAUGAHIDE. Mr. David Somerset. (*She steps* UP STAGE *as* DAVID ENTERS)

> (*On the soap* DAVID SOMERSET *plays a friendly neighbor cop and, like* DR. BROCK, *much of his television character spills over into real life*)

DAVID. Hi, citizens. No trouble, I hope.

OTHERS.
  Hi, David.
  Hello, David.
  Welcome.

MRS. NAUGAHIDE. I enjoy you so much on the program, Mr. Somerset. I only wish that when I was growing up we had a friendly neighborhood cop like you.

DAVID. That's nice of you to say so, Mrs. Tucker.

IVY. She's not Mrs. Tucker. Can't you see? She's wearing an apron.

LINK. This is Mrs. Naugafur, David.

MRS. NAUGAHIDE. Not *fur*. Hide. Naugahide. Think of imitation leather. (*To* DAVID) I cried real tears the day you rescued that kidnap victim who turned out to be your own long-lost sister.

DAVID. That episode did quite well in the ratings. (DOORBELL)

MRS. NAUGAHIDE. Busy night. (*She* EXITS LEFT. DAVID CROSSES CENTER)

DAVID. Never thought I'd see the inside of this place. (*Looks around*) High tone penthouse overlooking Times Square. I thought old man Tucker was a recluse.

DOTTIE. Not only that, he likes to keep to himself.

IVY. Please don't refer to H.T. as "Old Man Tucker." It's not respectful.

DAVID. I didn't see you sitting there, Robespierre.

ACT I   THE SOAPY MURDER CASE   19

Ivy. Miss Robespierre or Ivy M. Robespierre. Never—"Robespierre."

David. Sorry. I get so used to playing the cop that sometimes my speech sounds as if it comes off the hot sheet.

Link. What's the "M" stand for?

Jessica. Margaret?

Dottie. Mary? (*Pause*)

Ivy. Medea. (Mrs. Naugahide *returns*)

Mrs. Naugahide. Miss Mona La Mooch. (Mrs. Naugahide *steps* Up Stage)

(Mona Enters, *a "saintly mother" type. She carries a paper sack and is dressed plainly. Despite the warm summer night she wears a thin cloth coat with a ratty fur collar and a cheap little hat.* Note: Mona *wears this outfit during the entire play.* David *moves to chair beneath the portrait of* Horatio)

Mona. (*Holds up the paper sack*) I made some chicken soup for Mr. Tucker. It's my own recipe. I go heavy on the celery. (*She hands it to* Mrs. Naugahide)

Mrs. Naugahide. Isn't that thoughtful. Only Mr. Tucker is on a very strict diet. No greasy soup. (Mona *gives her a cold look.* Doorbell) I cried real tears when everyone thought you had drowned in the ice pond and went ahead with your funeral even though they didn't have a body. (Doorbell)

Mona. I always thought that was one of our better episodes.

Ivy. (*Grim-faced*) It got l-o-o-o-o-o-w ratings. (Mona *freezes, a look of agony on her face.* Ivy *does enjoy her authority and the effect it has on others. She smiles slyly, checks her fingernails, murmurs softly*) Chop, chop, chop. (*Others immediately react as* Mona *did.* Jessica *digs her nails into* Link's *arms*) I don't suppose there's any chopped liver about, Mrs. Naugahide? I could do with a bite.

Jessica. (*Stage whisper*) How about a cobra's (Doorbell)

Mrs. Naugahide. (*Returns paper sack*) Give it to him

yourself. I've suffered enough. (*She* EXITS LEFT. MONA *is bewildered by* MRS. NAUGAHIDE's *comment*)

MONA. What did she mean by that? (*She* CROSSES *to the fireplace and puts the package atop the mantel*)

DOTTIE. She seems to be the only servant here.

LINK. Mr. Tucker prefers his solitude.

DR. BROCK. I thought he lived out in the country somewhere.

DAVID. He does. Westchester County. Scarsdale, I think.

IVY. A man of H.T.'s wealth and reputation has many places of residence.

JESSICA. Has anyone actually met him?

DR. BROCK. Don't look at me.

MONA. I've never met him. I don't know anyone who has.

DAVID. Ditto.

IVY. I've met H.T.

DR. BROCK. Figures.

JESSICA. What sort of man is he?

IVY. Horatio Tucker is one of the most gentle, kind, soft-spoken men I have ever met. He's a great deal like myself.

HORATIO'S VOICE. (*Bellowing from* OFF RIGHT) *Mrs. Naugahide! I can't find my denture cream!*

MONA. What's that!

DR. BROCK. Sounds like someone in pain. I'll get my bag.

DAVID. More like a water buffalo stuck in a mudhole.

DOTTIE. It's Mr. Tucker. He's having trouble with his teeth. Last week he bit into a kaiser roll and it bit back. (MRS. NAUGAHIDE *returns*)

MRS. NAUGAHIDE. Mr. Phil Reinholt. (*She steps* UP STAGE. DR. BROCK *sits in the armchair*)

(PHIL REINHOLT ENTERS LEFT. *He plays the young man in the soap, college type. Wears glasses, a bow tie and V-neck sweater*)

PHIL. Not late am I?

ACT I   THE SOAPY MURDER CASE   21

Ivy. The invitation said eight o'clock. (*Checks wristwatch*) You have one minute and eleven seconds grace.

Phil. Got stuck in the subway.

David. Mechanical breakdown?

Phil. No, some kook painted the seats with glue.

Mrs. Naugahide. Oh, Phil Reinholt, I cried real tears the time the dean expelled you for cheating on your English Comprehension exam when, in reality, it was your rival for Dottie Duncan's affection who was the culprit. If it weren't for the support of Dr. Brock and saintly Mona La Mooch you might have left Pine Valley never to return.

Ivy. It's not necessary to repeat the plot of every episode, Mrs. Naugahide. We're all familiar with them.

Mrs. Naugahide. I do have to ask one thing. (*To* Phil) Will your courtship with Dottie end in marriage?

Link. Not on this show it won't.

Mrs. Naugahide. Then how will it end?

Phil. It won't end at all.

Jessica. Who ever heard of anything ending in a soap opera?

Horatio's Voice. *Mrs. Naugahide!*

Mrs. Naugahide. (Crosses Right) Now what's he up to? (Horatio *wheels himself in* Right. Mrs. Naugahide *steps behind the wheelchair. He indicates the area in front of the fireplace*)

Horatio. Over there! Push me over there! (*On his entrance everyone stands. Royalty has arrived.* Mrs. Naugahide *pushes him in front of the fireplace,* Down Stage *somewhat*) Sit down, sit down. (*Everyone who was previously sitting, sits again.* Phil *moves* Down Left. Mona *moves in front of table* Up Right)

Ivy. I don't believe you've met everyone, H.T. (*Indicates person as she makes the introduction*) Mona La Mooch, who plays Pine Valley's leading mother. Phil Reinholt, our college boy who has only one ambition in life—

Phil. To feel worthy and lovable, Mr. Tucker.

Horatio. Enough of this applesauce! You can fill me in later, Miss Robespierre.

Ivy. Whatever you say, H.T.

HORATIO. I want no scandal and I want no police interference. (*Others look to one another in amazement. What is he talking about?*)
LINK. What scandal, Mr. Tucker?
MONA. Did you say police?
HORATIO. I'm a rich man, a powerful man. I have enemies.
DOTTIE. That wouldn't include anyone here, Mr. Tucker.
HORATIO. Don't interrupt, Miss Coffee.
DOTTIE. Dunkin.
HORATIO. And don't correct me.
DAVID. What seems to be the problem, sir?
HORATIO. Someone is threatening to murder me.
AD LIBS.
  Murder!
  Who?
  You can't be serious!
  I can't believe it!
  (*Etc.*)
HORATIO. Cease! (*They fall silent. He takes a folded letter from some pocket*) The killer obviously has a perverse sense of humor. (*Shakes letter*) He—or she—or they—says I'll find a clue to my killer in television Episode Number 703.
LINK. That's tomorrow's episode.
HORATIO. A brilliant deduction, Kennecott. Especially since today's program was Episode Number 702. I have no intention of waiting until the new episode is taped in the morning. I'll see it tonight.
DR. BROCK. Tonight?
HORATIO. You've rehearsed it, haven't you?
MONA. Yes. This afternoon.
HORATIO. In that case, after dinner, you'll have no trouble in giving a little performance.
LINK. Someone's playing a joke.
MRS. NAUGAHIDE. People don't play jokes on Horatio Tucker.
HORATIO. Mrs. Naugahide, when I want your opinion I'll give it to you.
IVY. Why not simply read the script, H.T.? I have a copy in my attaché case.

HORATIO. Hate to read. Hurts my eyes.

PHIL. Someone could read it to you.

HORATIO. Can't abide being read to. (*Looks from one to the other*) We'll keep this little "matter" in the family. There has never been a breath of scandal with "Tucker's Tasty Pudding Powder And All-Purpose Detergent." It comes in fifth after the American flag, Mom, apple pie and Charlie Brown and the *Peanuts* gang. If news of what I just told you leaks out, I shall cancel "The Best Tears Of Our Lives." *Instantly*. (*All freeze in a tableau of mutual dismay*)

MRS. NAUGAHIDE. There won't be a dry eye in television land.

IVY. The threat of *murder* is more than a hint of scandal, H.T. Are you sure you don't want to involve the police?

HORATIO. No police. No outside interference. I'll handle this in my own way. I want to discover the clue to my "killer" myself. That's how I operate.

DR. BROCK. Speaking of operations, Link. I think we could whip up a dandy episode with me operating on a ship during a hurricane, and all the electricity goes and there's only candlelight and—

HORATIO. DON'T INTERRUPT! (DR. BROCK *cringes, slips lower and lower into his chair*) Once I discover my killer's identity, I'll deal with the rogue in my own fashion. I shall require the assistance of each and everyone of you. (*He goes into an almost operatic display of sneezing and coughing. Others stare, fascinated*)

DR. BROCK. (*Stands*) I'll get my bag.

HORATIO. Never mind your bag. You're like all the others. A quack. Get me to my room, Mrs. Naugahide. I want my bottle of phlegm dissolver.

MRS. NAUGAHIDE. (*Pushes him* RIGHT) Yes, sir.

HORATIO. You come along too, Miss Robespierre. I want a few words.

IVY. (*Stands*) Whatever you say, H.T. (*She* EXITS *after* HORATIO *and* MRS. NAUGAHIDE. DAVID *checks to ascertain that they're out of earshot*. LINK *stands, moves* CENTER)

LINK. If Mr. Tucker wants to cancel our show he can do it. He owns it.

JESSICA. It's the best job I've had!

MONA. It's the best job any of us have had.

PHIL. It's the only job I've had.

DR. BROCK. What am I going to do if the show is cancelled?

DOTTIE. There are always jobs for a doctor or a surgeon.

DR. BROCK. (*Furious*) You trying to be funny?

LINK. All right, everybody, keep calm. We'll do what Mr. Tucker wants. It's our only hope for survival.

MONA. (*Steps to* LINK) Why should anyone want to murder Tucker?

DAVID. You heard him. He's got enemies.

JESSICA. So has Ivy M. Robespierre, but no one's thought of doing her in.

DOTTIE. I've always wanted to poison Ivy.

DR. BROCK. Quiet! She might hear you.

MONA. She's destroyed so many careers.

JESSICA. Remember Lionel Shumway? When he fell in the ratings and was written out, he went to pieces.

LINK. Last time I saw him he was bumming spare change in Chinatown. I pretended I didn't know him. I was so embarrassed.

PHIL. I'll never forgive Miss Robespierre for Cecily Moonstone. Poor, poor Cecily. When her ratings fell off, and she was written out, she ended up giving garage sales, selling old jelly jars and picture frames.

DOTTIE. And poor Lottie Crummond. When she was written out she ended up going from door to door pushing used Avon products. (MRS. NAUGAHIDE *appears* RIGHT)

MRS. NAUGAHIDE. Punch on the garden terrace. Follow me, please. (*All, except* DR. BROCK *move to follow*)

JESSICA. This room reminds me of someplace I've been before.

LINK. I have the same feeling.

MONA. If Mr. Tucker is murdered where will that leave us?

DOTTIE. Standing in the unemployment line.
DAVID. I'll keep an eye on things. Don't forget I've got a policeman's brain.
PHIL. I'd like it better if you had a policeman's badge. (DR. BROCK *tiptoes to the hallway* RIGHT, *peers in to make certain they've all gone, then, fast, he races back to* IVY's *attaché case, opens it and begins to paw through the various papers*)
DR. BROCK. The new ratings report must be here. (*Frantic*) Where is it! (*He tosses papers aside, desperately searching*) Where? Where? (IVY *appears at the entryway* RIGHT, *plucks a flower from the floral arrangement. She watches* DR. BROCK *icily, then—*)
IVY. Perhaps, I could help you find what you're looking for, Dr. Brock.
DR. BROCK. (*Startled*) Auugh! (*He turns, fakes a smile*) Your attaché case fell over and all these papers fell out. (*He drops to one knee, grabs up the papers, stuffs them back into the attaché case.* IVY, *vampishly*, CROSSES *to him*)
IVY. You're a poor liar, Dr. Brock.
DR. BROCK. (*Nervously*) Liar?
IVY. You know perfectly well what you were looking for.
DR. BROCK. I do? (*He stands, puts attaché case on sofa*)
IVY. You want to see what everyone else wants to see. The latest report. (*Pause*) What you suspect is true.
DR. BROCK. (*Frightened*) I'm slipping in the ratings?
IVY. No.
DR. BROCK. That's a relief.
IVY. You've slipped.
DR. BROCK. (*About to break down*) You mean you're going to write me out. Me! Dr. Brock Rittenhouse! Solid, substantial, trustworthy?
IVY. (*Teases his chin with the flower*) Doesn't have to be that way, Dr. Brock.
DR. BROCK. What are you talking about, Miss Robespierre?
IVY. Call me Ivy.

Dr. Brock. Why?

Ivy. For one thing, it's my name.

Dr. Brock. But you don't like people to call you Ivy.

Ivy. I like you to call me Ivy. (*Passionately, she grabs at him*) You must have known how I felt about you. Couldn't you guess? I'm not all steel and wire. I am woman, flesh and blood. Kiss me. (*There's no escape for* Dr. Brock. Ivy *throws her arms around his neck and they go over in a backbend.* Ivy *plants a kiss. At that moment* Jessica *appears at the entryway* Right, *reacts, slaps her hands over her mouth to stifle an outcry, shaking her head from side to side as if what she's seeing couldn't possibly be true. Distressed, she flees*)

Dr. Brock. (*Freeing himself*) Someone might see us.

Ivy. What of it!

Dr. Brock. (*Nervous*) I better join the others. We don't want talk. (*He hurries* Right. Ivy *points an accusing finger*)

Ivy. Wait! (Dr. Brock *stops, turns*) I warn you! Don't trifle with my affections. I can keep you in soap or I can wash you out.

Dr. Brock. (*Calmly*) I'll remember that. (*He* Exits. Ivy *stares after him, not liking the tone of his voice. To business—*)

Ivy. Clue in Episode Number 703? (*Sits on sofa, opens attaché case, keeps flower in one hand*) If there's a clue in Episode Number 703 I'll find it. I *must* find it. (*She digs into the attaché case. As she does, there's activity with the portrait of* Horatio. *A long bamboo pole, like a large blowgun, is being slowly pushed from* Horatio's *mouth.* Ivy *pulls out the script*) Here it is. Episode Number 703! (*She stands, flips the pages*) What's the clue? What's the clue? (*As she flips the pages, the bamboo pole continues to grow in length. Finally, an "unseen" murder prop is projected.* Ivy *slaps at her neck*) Nasty mosquito. (*Quickly, the bamboo pole is withdrawn.* Ivy *flips a few more pages, feels the effect of the hit,* Screams! *The script drops from her hand. There's a look of utter disbelief on* Ivy's *face. Her eyes almost pop. She drops to*

ACT I THE SOAPY MURDER CASE 27

her knees. her hands clutching her throat. She can't breathe. She remains perfectly still for a moment and, then, with a spiralling moan, keels over sideways, rolls over on her back. The flower is still in her grip)

AD LIBS. (*From hallway,* RIGHT)
  Someone screamed!
  What is it!
  Sounded like a woman!
  Where's Miss Robespierre!
  (*Etc.*)
(*Like an unruly mob, everyone except* MRS. NAUGAHIDE *and* HORATIO *rush in*)

LINK. (*Spotting the body*) Look! A body on the carpet! (*They all crowd around*)

DAVID. I'll take charge. I'm a police officer.

MONA. Are you trying to be humorous? This could be serious.

DAVID. Better have a look at her, Dr. Brock.

DR. BROCK. Someone get my bag. Stand back. Give her air. (DOTTIE *moves to table* UP LEFT, *gets medical bag.* DR. BROCK *gets down on one knee, examines corpse*)

JESSICA. What can you tell?

DR. BROCK. One thing I can say with certainty.

PHIL. What?

DR. BROCK. It's Miss Robespierre.

LINK. (*Exasperated*) We know that. What's the matter with her?

DOTTIE. (*Pushes her way in*) Here's your medical bag, Dr. Brock.

DR. BROCK. Thanks, Dottie, but I won't be needing it. (*Dramatic pause*) She's gone.

MONA. You mean—she's dead?

DR. BROCK. She'll never be deader.

DOTTIE. She may be dead, but at least she's neat about it. Look—she died with a flower in her hand.

DR. BROCK. There's only one thing lower than *her* ratings now.

JESSICA. What?

DR. BROCK. (*Seriously*) Her grave. (*They stare down at* IVY *not quite believing she's kaput.* MRS. NAUGAHIDE, *a starched white cap on her head,* ENTERS RIGHT. *She carries a dinner gong and hammer*)

MRS. NAUGAHIDE. (*Cheerily*) Dinner is served. (*She strikes the gong*)

Fast Curtain

END OF ACT ONE

ACT TWO

TIME: *Later.*

AT RISE: JESSICA *stands by the entryway,* LEFT, *looking* OFF STAGE *toward the unseen library.* MONA *sits on sofa;* DOTTIE *at the fireplace. They too, are looking* LEFT. *Sack containing the chicken soup, and the attaché case, have been struck.*

MONA. Poor Mr. Tucker. His dinner party was ruined. It's not pleasant finding a corpse on the carpet.

DOTTIE. I lost my appetite. Couldn't eat a thing at the table.

MONA. You may feel like nibbling later on.

DOTTIE. Why are they taking so long?

JESSICA. Dr. Brock is performing the autopsy.

DOTTIE. He could lose his license.

JESSICA. He doesn't have a license.

MONA. When it comes to autopsies, Dr. Brock is nothing more than a talented amateur.

DOTTIE. Why put Miss Robespierre's body in the library?

MONA. Why not put it in the library?

JESSICA. Good a place as any.

DOTTIE. Why not put it out on the garden terrace? It's cooler. Besides, who wants to go for a book and find a stiff.

MONA. Such language! Where did a sweet young thing like you learn such an expression? "Go for a book and find a stiff." Tsk, tsk.

DOTTIE. (*Moves behind table*) I'm upset. I only meant that I think the garden terrace is a better place than the library.

JESSICA. A helicopter advertising a discotheque might fly over.

Mona. Or one of those blimps that advertise suntan lotion. The sky is cluttered with them.

Jessica. A body on the garden terrace would look suspicious.

Dottie. Not if you prop Miss Robespierre up in a lounge chair, put a magazine in her hand and a box of chocolates in her lap.

Mona. You surprise me, Dottie. That's a rather clever suggestion.

Jessica. She'd hardly be reading a magazine in the dark. Besides, I think the library is poetic justice. Ivy M. Robespierre wasn't exactly the "good literature" type.

Dottie. We could get into trouble.

Mona. We're already in trouble.

Jessica. Our television show could be cancelled at any moment.

Mona. "The Best Tears Of Our Lives" is my last chance for security and I know it.

Dottie. We're accessories after the fact. Maybe before the fact.

Mona. What fact?

Dottie. The murder.

Jessica. Mr. Tucker hasn't been murdered yet. That's why we're here in his fashionable mid-town penthouse.

Mona. To discover who's *trying* to murder him.

Dottie. I'm not talking about Mr. Tucker. I mean Ivy. She's the one who's been murdered.

Mona. What an odd thing to say.

Jessica. Who says she's been murdered?

Dottie. Hasn't she?

Jessica. (*Stepping into room*) Simply because she was found on the carpet with a flower in her hand, and was a perfectly despicable person hated by the hundreds of people who knew her, is no reason to suspect foul play. For all we know, Ivy might have died of a heart condition.

Mona. Impossible.

Jessica. Why do you say that?

Mona. Miss Robespierre didn't have a heart.

Jessica. Now you're trying to be clever.

MONA. Not in the least. However, I see no reason not to appreciate the practical side of all this.

JESSICA. *Practical* side?

MONA. Don't you see? With Ivy M. Robespierre out of the way, our lives will be easier. She won't be breathing down our necks.

JESSICA. The network is bound to replace her.

MONA. Yes, but Ivy was one of a kind. Unique. No one else could be quite like her. Whoever replaces her is bound to have more humanity. (JESSICA *steps to armchair*)

JESSICA. I know Link will be delighted she's gone. Oh, he won't say anything. He'll be delighted nonetheless.

MONA. Because she won't be around to harrass him?

JESSICA. (*With hidden meaning*) For a better reason than that.

MONA. (*Interested*) You know something? Something about Ivy and Link?

JESSICA. Maybe I do, maybe I don't.

DOTTIE. My mother was right. I should have gone straight instead of becoming an actress.

MONA. *Gone straight?* You shouldn't use slang expressions. As a cast member of "The Best Tears Of Our Lives" you have to set an example for the public.

DOTTIE. I had other ambitions, but mother was on the stage. I wanted to be just like her.

JESSICA. You're lucky your mother wasn't a bearded lady. (*Sits in armchair.* PHIL ENTERS LEFT)

PHIL. Guess what!

OTHERS. What?

PHIL. Dr. Brock says she was poisoned. (*Women tense*) You know how he is about medicine and things. He's better than a real doctor.

DOTTIE. What kind of poison?

PHIL. The kind that kills.

MONA. In something she ate?

JESSICA. In something she drank?

DOTTIE. In something she didn't eat or drink?

PHIL. He found a poisoned thumb tack stuck in her neck.

MONA. Thumb tack?

JESSICA. That's ridiculous. (DR. BROCK ENTERS LEFT. *In keeping with his "method" acting he wears a surgical mask and is stripping off a pair of surgical gloves*)

PHIL. Ask him yourself. (PHIL *moves* DOWN LEFT. DR. BROCK CROSSES CENTER, *unties mask*)

DR. BROCK. (*Seriously*) In all my years living here in Pine Valley I've never run across a case like this.

MONA. What are you talking about? This isn't Pine Valley.

JESSICA. We're in mid-town New York.

DOTTIE. This is real life.

PHIL. (*Gloomily*) Murder's a part of it.

DR. BROCK. You have to understand my position. The only way I can create my character is to live the role—

MONA. (*Sighs*) Day and night, night and day.

DR. BROCK. (*Pulls up his trousers' legs to display his vivid red socks*) When I first came to Manhattan I thought I'd create an image casting directors and agents would never forget. I would be known as the actor who always wears red socks.

PHIL. Instead of that, people think you never change your socks.

DR. BROCK. That's enough out of you, Phil. Don't forget I get more fan mail than all other members of the cast *combined*.

JESSICA. Let's forget about those red socks.

PHIL. That won't be easy.

MONA. Never mind your image. What about Ivy M. Robespierre?

DR. BROCK. She's dead.

JESSICA. We know that!

MONA. What about the autopsy! (DAVID ENTERS LEFT. *He wears a policeman's hat, jacket*)

DAVID. Dr. Brock says it was "snakeroot."

DOTTIE. What are you wearing?

JESSICA. It's your costume from the soap, isn't it?

DAVID. I had it in the hallway with my dirty laundry. I was going to stop off at the cleaners after dinner. (*A touch embarrassed*) I thought since this is a homicide, I ought to change. If Dr. Brock can do his thing I don't see why I can't do mine. Fair's fair.

ACT II THE SOAPY MURDER CASE 33

Mona. I never heard of anything so childish.

David. It is not childish. Look at you. You're never out of that seedy cloth coat with the ratty fur collar and that mean little hat.

Mona. (*Touches her hat, offended*) Oh!

David. If you can play at being saintly Mother La Mooch, I don't see why I can't play at being Officer Somerset. I can solve this case with one eye tied behind my back.

Jessica. This is no time for any of us to be playing. You said "homicide."

David. Yeah. The snakeroot.

Dr. Brock. Definitely snakeroot.

Mona. (*Awed*) Imagine—snakeroot.

Jessica. Snakeroot? Who would have thought it?

Dottie. The killer.

Mona. I have a question.

David. Shoot.

Mona. What's snakeroot?

Dr. Brock. It's a wild flower. Abraham Lincoln's mother died by drinking milk from a cow that grazed on snakeroot. (Horatio's Voice *is heard from* Off Right. *All look*)

Horatio's Voice. I insist we deal with this matter my way.

Link's Voice. (*Protesting*) Mr. Tucker, it's against the law. We're breaking the law. (Mrs. Naugahide *pushes* Horatio *in his wheelchair. She wheels him* Down Right. Link *follows in, stands behind table.* Dialogue *through this blocking*)

Horatio. Applesauce! Applesauce! I'm the law! If I say we deal with this matter my way—I mean we deal with this matter MY WAY!

Mrs. Naugahide. You're repeating yourself.

Horatio. I only repeat myself when I eat radishes.

Dottie. (*Sits*) She was *murdered*, Mr. Tucker.

Horatio. Who?

Phil. The only corpse in the penthouse. (*Thinks*) I hope.

Jessica. Miss Robespierre.

HORATIO. Murdered? Rubbish. A stroke of some sort. Heart attack. Embolism.

DR. BROCK. I'm afraid not, Mr. Tucker.

HORATIO. I'm the one who's supposed to get murdered, not Miss Robespierre.

JESSICA. The best laid plans of mice and men—

HORATIO. I'm not talking about mice and I'm not talking about men—

MONA. It was snakeroot.

MRS. NAUGAHIDE. Snakeroot who?

HORATIO. (*To* LINK) Do we have someone on the payroll named Snakeroot?

LINK. I don't recognize the name.

PHIL. It's not a person. It's a poison.

MONA. Same thing that killed Abraham Lincoln's mother.

HORATIO. What has Abraham Lincoln's mother got to do with a threat on my life? You're a bunch of Looney Tunes.

DR. BROCK (*Leans against mantel*) Snakeroot is a little known plant poison. Deadly, fatal, final.

MRS. NAUGAHIDE. Why would she drink something like that?

MONA. Wait a minute. We all drank the same thing.

PHIL. The punch.

MRS. NAUGAHIDE. (*Insulted*) There were no snakes or roots in my punch!

DOTTIE. Miss Robespierre wasn't with us on the terrace.

DAVID. (*Takes command*) I think things will go faster if I handle this case. Don't forget, people, David Somerset is trained for police work.

HORATIO. (*To* MRS. NAUGAHIDE) What's he wearing?

MRS. NAUGAHIDE. Looks like some sort of police uniform.

LINK. It's the costume he wears on the soap.

HORATIO. Where did he get it?

PHIL. From his dirty laundry. In the hallway.

HORATIO. (*Growls*) My hallway is not a laundromat, and the only dirty laundry I'm interested in is my own. Who is out to kill me and why? That's all that matters.

DAVID. (*Moves* CENTER) The autopsy shows that the

ACT II   THE SOAPY MURDER CASE   35

Robespierre dame died as a result of a poisoned thumb tack.

DOTTIE. Poor Mrs. Lincoln.

HORATIO. What autopsy?

DR. BROCK. Let me explain—

HORATIO. Shut up! (*To* DAVID) Get on with it.

DAVID. She didn't drink the thumb tack.

HORATIO. (*Sarcastic*) Amazing.

DAVID. Somebody threw it at her with considerable force.

HORATIO. Who?

DAVID. Who was the last person to see her alive?

MRS. NAUGAHIDE. She was with Mr. Tucker and I, but she left.

DAVID. Why?

MRS. NAUGAHIDE. She said she was going to get her attaché case.

DAVID. Then she must have met somebody in this room. But who? Who! (*Nervously, all look from one to the other*)

MONA. Who?

JESSICA. Who? (*She gives* DR. BROCK *an icy glare*)

DR. BROCK. Who?

HORATIO. Never mind all this talk about who! If Miss Robespierre was murdered it only goes to prove that I'm in imminent danger.

MRS. NAUGAHIDE. (*An idea strikes*) I think I have it.

HORATIO. Don't stand too close. You know I'm allergic to almost everything.

MRS. NAUGAHIDE. The killer must have mistaken Miss Robespierre for Mr. Tucker.

JESSICA. What a simpleton.

HORATIO. (*Conceited*) I hardly think anyone would mistake me for Miss Robespierre. For one thing, even though I'm older I'm better looking.

DAVID. It's "murder-most-foul," like they say in Shakespeare, Mr. Tucker.

HORATIO. Let's forget Shakespeare and let's forget Abraham Lincoln's mother. I suggest we get on with Episode Number 703. When we find the clue we'll undoubtedly discover the murderer of Miss Robespierre.

I'm counting on your loyalty to "Tucker's Tasty Pudding Powder and All-Purpose Detergent."

DAVID. I think I can prove our loyalty, Mr. Tucker. (*Takes out a key, holds it up*)

HORATIO. What's that?

DAVID. I got this in the library. It was on your desk. The key to the front door.

MRS. NAUGAHIDE. (CROSSES *over, checks*) So it is.

LINK. So what?

DAVID. None of us will leave this apartment until the killer is caught. (*Puts key in his mouth*)

MONA. What are you doing with that key!

DAVID. (*Swallows*) Gulp.

LINK. He's swallowed it!

JESSICA. That's how you prove our loyalty?

HORATIO. Numbskull! The front door can't be locked from the inside. Only from the outside.

MRS. NAUGAHIDE. There's a double-bolt on the inside. Maybe you could swallow that.

DAVID. (*Rubs his neck, an odd expression on his face*) I wonder if I could have a glass of water?

MRS. NAUGAHIDE. (*Indicates table* UP RIGHT) On the table there. (DAVID CROSSES *to table, pours a glass of water from a decanter, drinks.* DIALOGUE *through*)

LINK. I must say something, Mr. Tucker.

HORATIO. I'm listening.

LINK. Apparently *murder* has been committed.

DR. BROCK. You have my word on that. Snakeroot.

LINK. I'm willing to go along with the presentation of Episode Number 703, but I think we ought to give our cast one last opportunity to back out. (HORATIO *looks fierce*)

HORATIO. (*The phlegm rattling in his throat*) You mean there might be someone who doesn't want to go along with my wishes? (*Eyes narrow as he scans the room*) Who?

MRS. NAUGAHIDE. We're back to who again.

MONA. I'm happy to do as you suggest, sir. I'm sure we all are.

AD-LIBS.
   Yes!

Absolutely!
Positively!
A pleasure.
(*Etc.*)

HORATIO. (*Settles back in his wheelchair, pleased that he's gotten his way*) What do you say to that, Kennecott?

LINK. I say—bubble on.

HORATIO. (*Wringing his hands in delight*) Splendid. We'll find the clue together.

DOTTIE. What will we use for tomorrow's set?

LINK. (*Looks around*) This room would be perfect. (*Points*) Everything's here for Jessica Courtney's penthouse apartment. (*Points*) There's our fireplace . . . sofa . . . armchair . . . table.

PHIL. What about props?

LINK. We'll pantomime, or improvise.

JESSICA. The mood won't be the same.

MONA. The lighting isn't anything like what we have at the studio.

HORATIO. Take care of that, Mrs. Naugahide. (*She steps to portrait, snaps on some switch.* INSTANTLY, *for comic effect, the stage lighting becomes the same as it would be at the television studio. Theatrical, artificial, concentrated in the* CENTER *of the room.* HORATIO *is in the shadows. Others look about, amazed*)

PHIL. Wow!

DOTTIE. It's like the studio lighting we have every day.

HORATIO. When you're rich like me you can have anything you want.

LINK. They may not be letter-perfect, Mr. Tucker. In the studio we use idiot cards.

HORATIO. Mrs. Naugahide will be your idiot.

MRS. NAUGAHIDE. I don't want to be anyone's idiot. Sounds worse than being a barometer or a figure of speech.

LINK. No, no, you don't understand. We have the words written out on large placards in case anyone forgets his lines. He simply looks off camera and there's his dialogue.

JESSICA. We hardly ever use them.

HORATIO. Then there's no reason for delay. Get moving, Kennecott. (LINK *moves* CENTER, *plucks a script from his back pocket*)
LINK. We come in with a tight shot of Mother La Mooch at the fireplace.
HORATIO. That's *exactly* how the episode will begin?
LINK. Not exactly.
HORATIO. I want it *exactly*.
LINK. (*To "Best Tears" cast members*) Places.

(PHIL *and* JESSICA EXIT LEFT. DOTTIE, DAVID *and* DR. BROCK EXIT RIGHT. MONA *moves to the fireplace.* MRS. NAUGAHIDE *wheels* HORATIO *further* DOWN RIGHT, *so attention is riveted on the "stagey lighting area."* MRS. NAUGAHIDE *sits on chair,* DOWN RIGHT *of hallway.* NOTE: *What we will be watching is an episode of "The Best Tears Of Our Lives." In true soap opera fashion, the acting will be understated, muted. The plotting ridiculous*)

MRS. NAUGAHIDE. This *is* a tasty treat, Mr. Tucker. What a pity Miss Robespierre has to miss it.
LINK. We open with a few bars of taped organ music. It's an idea I never liked, but Miss Robespierre thought it might appeal to the nostalgia buffs. Older viewers would be able to identify, those who grew up on radio.
HORATIO. She knew her job.
LINK. (*Dislikes the observation*) Yes. (*Clears his throat again*) I'll take the announcer's part.
HORATIO. One moment. (*Turns his head*) Mrs. Naugahide. (*She gets up, moves to portrait and presses another button.* SOFT ORGAN MUSIC PLAYS. MRS. NAUGAHIDE *returns to her chair.* LINK *and* MONA *are impressed.* PHIL *sticks his head in,* LEFT)
PHIL. Wow, Mr. Tucker! Organ music and everything! Fantastic! (*He ducks back into hallway. With the syrupy* ORGAN MUSIC PLAYING *in background,* LINK *takes on the role of television announcer*)
LINK. GOOD AFTERNOON, TELEVISION FANS.
MRS. NAUGAHIDE. Good afternoon.
HORATIO. Sssshhh.

ACT II THE SOAPY MURDER CASE 39

LINK. "TUCKER'S TASTY PUDDING POWDER AND ALL-PURPOSE DETERGENT" IS PROUD TO BRING YOU ANOTHER EPISODE OF "THE BEST TEARS OF OUR LIVES."

HORATIO. So far it's terrible.

LINK. (*Pressing on*) A TRUE-TO-LIFE TELEVISION DRAMA OF EXCEPTIONAL QUALITY THAT ASKS THE QUESTION, "CAN A BEAUTIFUL YOUNG STEPMOTHER AND FORMER NURSE, CAN A WIDOW WITH ELEVEN CHILDREN, CAN A RESTLESS AIRLINE STEWARDESS MARRIED TO A PREOCCUPIED DENTIST, CAN A CAREFREE MOUNTAIN WOMAN IN LOVE WITH AN ARAB BILLIONAIRE, CAN A WOMAN MARRIED TO AN AMNESIA CASE—CAN THEY FIND HAPPINESS IN THE SUBURBAN COMMUNITY OF PLEASANT PINE VALLEY?" (*He pauses*)

HORATIO. What are you waiting for?

LINK. At this point we have a commercial.

HORATIO. Then the episode?

LINK. No. Another commercial.

HORATIO. *Then* the episode.

LINK. No. Another commercial. Then we begin. (*As television announcer*) WE OPEN EPISODE NUMBER 703 AS SAINTLY MOTHER LA MOOCH PAYS A VISIT TO THE PENTHOUSE APARTMENT OF GLAMOROUS, BUT EVIL, JESSICA COURTNEY, RICHEST WOMAN IN PLEASANT PINE VALLEY. (LINK *moves* UP LEFT. ORGAN MUSIC OUT. MONA *moves* DOWN STAGE, *fussing with her ratty fur collar, nervous*)

MONA. (*Into her "soap" role*) PERHAPS IT WAS A MISTAKE COMING HERE. (*False laughter from* JESSICA OFF STAGE LEFT)

JESSICA. HA. HA. HA. (*She* ENTERS, *poses dramatically at the entryway*)

MONA. WHY ARE YOU LAUGHING LIKE THAT, MISS COURTNEY?

JESSICA. BECAUSE I KNEW ONE DAY YOU WOULD PAY ME A VISIT, MOTHER LA MOOCH. IF I WAITED LONG ENOUGH. (*She* CROSSES *to sofa, sits*) I KNOW WHY YOU'RE HERE. YOU'RE WASTING YOUR TIME.

MONA. (*Holds out her hands as if she were offering some gift*) THIS IS FOR YOU.

JESSICA. (*Takes "it," looks at "it"*) WHAT IS IT?

MONA. HOME MADE CHICKEN SOUP. I WENT HEAVY ON THE CELERY.

JESSICA. HERE'S WHAT I THINK OF YOUR CHICKEN SOUP. (*Tosses "soup" over her shoulder*) HA. HA. HA.

MONA. (*Runs behind sofa*) ALL OVER YOUR BEAUTIFUL EXPENSIVE CARPET.

JESSICA. THE MAID WILL CLEAN IT UP.

MONA. WHY DO YOU HATE ME?

JESSICA. DO I HATE YOU?

MONA. YES, YOU HATE ME.

JESSICA. IF YOU SAY SO. I HATE YOU.

MONA. WHY HAVE YOU STOPPED THE BANK FROM ADVANCING ME MONEY FOR MY OPERATION?

JESSICA. I HAVE MY REASONS.

MONA. WITHOUT THAT OPERATION MY EYES WON'T BE MUCH GOOD.

JESSICA. YOU'VE COME HERE UNINVITED AND SPOILED MY LUNCH.

MONA. WHY ARE YOU DOING THIS? WHY? WHY?

JESSICA. (*Stands, faces her*) WHY, WHY? I'LL TELL YOU WHY.

MONA. YES, TELL ME WHY?

JESSICA. HERE'S WHY. BECAUSE YOU STOLE THE ONLY MAN I EVER LOVED. YOU'LL NEVER GET YOUR OPERATION. NOT AS LONG AS I CONTROL THE BANK.

DOTTIE. (ENTERS RIGHT) DO YOU WANT ANYTHING, MISS COURTNEY?

MONA. DOTTIE DUNCAN, YOU HERE?

JESSICA. I'VE HIRED HER AS A MAID. (*Points*) CLEAN UP THAT CHICKEN SOUP.

DOTTIE. YES, MA'AM. (DOTTIE *goes behind sofa, gets down on her knees, pretends to clean up*)

MONA. I DON'T UNDERSTAND.
DOTTIE. (*Cleaning, cleaning*) I HAVE TO RAISE MONEY FOR PHIL. HE NEEDS A LAWYER.
MONA. PHIL REINHOLT? WHAT'S HE DONE?
PHIL. (ENTERS LEFT) LET ME ANSWER THAT, MOTHER LA MOOCH.
DOTTIE. YES, PHIL. YOU ANSWER IT.
PHIL. I WILL ANSWER IT. I'VE BEEN UNJUSTLY ACCUSED OF STEALING MY FRATERNITY'S REFRIGERATOR. PHI ALPHA MOO MOO HAS NO PLACE TO STORE ITS BEER.
DOTTIE. HE'S INNOCENT.
PHIL. I'M INNOCENT.
MONA. I BELIEVE YOU'RE INNOCENT.
JESSICA. IF YOU MUST VISIT ONE OF MY SERVANTS, DO IT IN THE KITCHEN.
DOTTIE. (*Cleaning, cleaning*) THIS CHICKEN SOUP IS GREASY.
DAVID. (ENTERS RIGHT) I CAME IN THE BACK WAY, MISS COURTNEY. I SAW PHIL REINHOLT COME UP IN THE ELEVATOR. FIGURED HE'D MIGHT BE UP TO NO GOOD.
PHIL. I'M NOT A CROOK.
DOTTIE. (*Cleaning, cleaning*) SHE WENT AWFUL HEAVY ON THE CELERY.
JESSICA. (*To* MONA) I HAVE A GUEST. YOU'VE COME AT AN INCONVENIENT TIME.
PHIL. WHAT'S GOING TO HAPPEN TO ME?
DOTTIE. DON'T WORRY, PHIL. AS LONG AS YOU HAVE ME, YOU HAVE HOPE.
PHIL. I HOPE SO, DOTTIE.
JESSICA. I WONDER WHY YOU DON'T GET BORED LIVING IN PLEASANT PINE VALLEY, DOTTIE? A YOUNG GIRL LIKE YOU. YOU NEED EXCITEMENT.
DOTTIE. (*Looks up, an angelic look on her face*) EXCITEMENT IS ONE THING. REAL FEELINGS ARE ANOTHER. HERE IN PLEASANT PINE VALLEY, WE KNOW HOW TO FEEL.
MONA. YOU'RE RICH, DOTTIE DUNCAN, AND YOU DON'T KNOW IT.

David. COME ALONG, REINHOLT. I WANT A WORD WITH YOU. (*He* Crosses Left, *collars* Phil)

Phil. I'M BEING TREATED LIKE A CRIMINAL. I'M BEING FRAMED.

David. THE JURY WILL DECIDE THAT.

Dottie. PHIL! (Dottie *follows after* David *and* Phil, Left. Dr. Brock Enters Right)

Mona. I'VE BEEN A WIDOW FOR YEARS, JESSICA. WHAT'S DONE IS DONE. YOU HAVE EVERYTHING. I HAVE NOTHING. ISN'T THAT VICTORY ENOUGH?

Jessica. POO.

Dr. Brock. ANYTHING THE MATTER?

Mona. DR. BROCK—YOU. HERE.

Dr. Brock. I'M HAVING LUNCH WITH JESSICA. (*Suddenly,* Jessica *jumps* out of character *and verbally attacks* Dr. Brock *with a vengeance*)

Jessica. I saw you with Ivy! You can't fool me! (Mona *and* Dr. Brock *are shocked*. Phil *flips pages in his script*)

Link. Wait a minute. That's not in the script.

Horatio. It was the only part I liked.

Jessica. (*Gets control of herself*) I am sorry. I got my lines all mixed up. (*Back into "soap" character*) NOTHING'S THE MATTER, DR. BROCK.

Mona. EXCEPT I DON'T GET THE MONEY FOR MY OPERATION.

Dr. Brock. (*Chest out*) DON'T WORRY ABOUT THAT, MOTHER LA MOOCH. I'LL SEE THAT YOU GET IT. YOU CAN RELY ON DR. BROCK RITTENHOUSE.

Mona. BLESS YOU.

Dr. Brock. THIS HAS GONE ON TOO LONG, JESSICA.

Horatio. I agree. (*They ignore him, continue*)

Jessica. WHAT HAS GONE ON TOO LONG, DR. BROCK?

Dr. Brock. YOU WERE BOTH ORPHANS.

Mona. I KNOW THAT. JESSICA KNOWS THAT. YOU KNOW THAT. EVERYBODY KNOWS THAT.

ACT II   THE SOAPY MURDER CASE   43

DR. BROCK. YES, BUT I KNOW SOMETHING THAT YOU DON'T KNOW.

JESSICA. WHAT?

MONA. WHAT?

MRS. NAUGAHIDE. What?

DR. BROCK. THE PROOF IS IN A SEALED ENVELOPE AT PINE VALLEY CITY HOSPITAL. YOU ARE— (*Long dramatic pause*) —SISTERS!

OTHERS. SISTERS!

DR. BROCK. RAISED BY DIFFERENT PARENTS, BUT SISTERS ALL THE SAME.

JESSICA. (*Starts to cry, sits on sofa*) WHAT A REVELATION! I'M SO ASHAMED. MONA, SIT BESIDE ME. (MONA *does.* JESSICA *takes her hand*) I'M NOT REALLY AN EVIL PERSON. TRUE, I'M THE RICHEST WOMAN IN TOWN, BUT I CAN'T HELP THAT. I BELIEVE ONE CAN BE A GOOD PERSON AND INCREDIBLY WEALTHY AT THE SAME TIME. WE WILL HAVE TO GET TO KNOW EACH OTHER, MOTHER LA MOOCH, OR MAY I CALL YOU . . . SISTER?

MONA. (*Pause*) DO I GET MY OPERATION? (DR. BROCK, MONA, JESSICA *freeze.* LINK *moves down behind the armchair*)

LINK. (*The announcer*) DON'T MISS TOMORROW'S EPISODE NUMBER 704, WHEN PHIL REINHOLT IS FREED FROM SUSPICION, DR. BROCK IS FIRED FOR REVEALING THE CONTENTS OF PRIVATE HOSPITAL FILES, DOTTIE DUNCAN IS KIDNAPPED BY GYPSIES AND MOTHER LA MOOCH STRUGGLES WITH THE QUESTION—"CAN A SAINTLY WOMAN IN SUBURBAN PLEASANT PINE VALLEY LIVE AND FORGIVE?" (BLAST *of* ORGAN MUSIC *signals the end*)

HORATIO. A program like that gives virtue a bad name. You certainly have the courage of your cliches, Kennecott. That's what I've been paying for? Mishmash! Applesauce!

LINK. You didn't like it?

HORATIO. Lumpy and brief. The brief part is the best I can say for it.

MRS. NAUGAHIDE. Seems longer on television.
JESSICA. We speak much slower.
MONA. Much, much slower.
DR. BROCK. There are more commercials.
HORATIO. That was the episode? *Exactly?*
LINK. Definitely, Mr. Tucker.
HORATIO. That's *exactly* the way it will be taped in the morning?
LINK. Word for word.
MONA. You're mistaken, Link.
LINK. How so?
MONA. That little outburst Jessica made against Dr. Brock. I can recall her exact words. (*Recalls*) "I saw you with Ivy. You can't fool me."
HORATIO. (*Delighted*) That's right! That's right! That must be the clue!
LINK. What did you mean by that, Jessica?
JESSICA. (*Upset, she stands*) I simply forgot my lines.
HORATIO. Nonsense!
JESSICA. All right, I'll tell you!

(FAST BLACKOUT. DOTTIE SCREAMS *from* OFF STAGE LEFT. MRS. NAUGAHIDE SCREAMS *in the blackness.* SOUND *of* PISTOL *being* FIRED! *Once—Twice—Three times!* JESSICA SCREAMS)

LINK. (*In blackout*) What's going on!
MRS. NAUGAHIDE. Help!

(*Scene returns to* GENERAL STAGE LIGHTING, *as in opening of act.* DR. BROCK *is gone;* JESSICA *is stretched out on the floor in front of sofa. No one notices her, nor do they notice the dagger that's plunged into the armchair, pinning down an envelope.* DAVID, DOTTIE *and* PHIL *stand at entryway* LEFT)

MRS. NAUGAHIDE. (*Stands*) Con Edison has done it again.
MONA. Done what?
MRS. NAUGAHIDE. Every summer the same thing.
LINK. You mean the blackout?

MRS. NAUGAHIDE. Air-conditioners and what-not overload the circuits and we have blackout after blackout. I suppose next there'll be a garbage strike, or the newspapers will cease to publish, or the subway will stop running. (HORATIO *is seething at their indifference to the "gunshots" and their idle conversation*)

LINK. Still, there's no place like New York for intellectual stimulation.

MRS. NAUGAHIDE. Or the Broadway shows. I like the musicals best of all, especially if there's an overture.

PHIL. I couldn't live anyplace else.

LINK. After New York it's all desert.

MONA. New York is Fun City. (*Finally, HORATIO explodes, beats his fists on the arms of the wheelchair, thrashes about almost violently*)

HORATIO. Auuuuuuugh!

MRS. NAUGAHIDE. (*Steps close*) Mr. Tucker, what's wrong?

HORATIO. You banana brains! Talking Chamber of Commerce applesauce when I might have been killed by a bullet!

LINK. (*Recalls*) I did hear gunfire!

MONA. So did I.

DAVID. (*Moves behind sofa*) Probably a car backfiring.

HORATIO. How would we be able to hear it sixty floors up! (DAVID *scratches his head. He doesn't know*)

DOTTIE. (*Sees JESSICA*) What's the matter with her?

MRS. NAUGAHIDE. Who?

DOTTIE. On the carpet. Looks like Jessica Courtney. (MONA *notices, gives a muffled scream, jumps up*)

HORATIO. Aha! The bullets got her by mistake.

JESSICA. (*Coming to*) I'm all right . . . fainted in the excitement . . . (*Quickly everyone becomes agitated, ignoring her words*)

PHIL. Where's Dr. Brock?

DAVID. She's unconscious. I'll give her cardio-pulmonary resuscitation. (*Action goes into high gear,* DIALOGUE *overlapping. Feebly,* JESSICA *attempts to protest that she's only fainted, but the others are convinced she's been shot*)

Mrs. Naugahide. Why would anyone want to shoot poor Jessica Courtney?

David. (*Hurries to her, drops to one knee*) Someone get some water!

Dottie. I'll get it! (Crosses *to water decanter on* Up Right *table*)

Mrs. Naugahide. I'll get a damp towel. (*She* Exits Right. Link *and* Phil *move to the body as* David *tilts* Jessica's *head back and attempts to inflate her lungs*)

Mona. Calling Dr. Brock! Calling Dr. Brock! Emergency!

Jessica. I'm all right . . .

Link. Is she still alive, David?

Mr. Tucker. (*Happy*) The killer missed me again! Ha! Ha! Ha! (Jessica *is suffocating with* David's *clumsy attempts to revive her*)

Link. Does she have a pulse?

Mona. I'll try acupuncture!

Horatio. Acupuncture! (Jessica *is struggling to push* David *away*. Mona *plucks a pin from her hat, jabs* Jessica *in the hip*)

Jessica. OOOOOOOOOW! (*She sits up just as* Dottie *runs down to her and throws a glass of water in her face*. Jessica *is infuriated*) WHAT ARE YOU DOING!

David. We thought you were shot.

Jessica. Shot where?

David In the blackout. (*He helps her up*)

Jessica. I wasn't shot! I fainted! (Dottie *returns the glass to table*)

Link. Whoever is after you, Mr. Tucker, has trouble finding the target.

Horatio. You sound disappointed, Kennecott.

Mona. (*Notices dagger and note stuck in armchair*) What's that?

David. Where?

Mona. (*Points*) Stuck in the armchair. (*All except* Horatio *crowd around armchair*)

Horatio. (*Impatient*) What is it? What is it? Tell me.

Jessica. Whatever it is, it wasn't there before the blackout.

Mona. It's a dagger.

ACT II   THE SOAPY MURDER CASE   47

HORATIO. (*Worried*) Dagger?
DOTTIE. With an envelope.
HORATIO. Envelope?
LINK. There's writing on it.
HORATIO. Writing?
DOTTIE. There's an echo in here.
HORATIO. (*Wheels himself in front of the table*) Are you just going to stare at that envelope?!
DAVID. Better let me see it first. This is a police matter. (*Takes out dagger, studies envelope*)
MONA. What does it say?
DAVID. It's addressed to someone.
LINK. This could be important.
HORATIO. (*Shaking with emotion*) Who's it addressed to? Who?
OTHERS. Who? Who?
DAVID. (*Studies the name of the addressee*) Not who—whom. "To Whom It May Concern."
JESSICA. Open it.
MONA. Read it.
DAVID. (*Opens envelope, takes out a sheet of paper, scans contents*) Unbelievable . . . unbelievable . . . unbelievable . . .
LINK. (*Grabs sheet of paper*) Let me see that. (*Reads*) "I've written this confession . . ."
DOTTIE. Confession!
HORATIO. Now we're getting somewhere.
LINK. "I've written this confession because I don't want anyone to be blamed for the murder of Ivy M. Robespierre. I alone am guilty. She knew that I was none other than the infamous Doctor Fingers . . ."
OTHERS. Doctor Fingers!
LINK. "She was blackmailing me and there's only one way to deal with blackmailers. You'll never see me again. Good luck with the soap. Keep it clean." It's signed "Brock Rittenhouse, A.K.A., Dr. Fingers."
DOTTIE. A.K.A.?
LINK. Also Known As.
JESSICA. (*Recalls*) I remember that name. It was a famous case many years ago.
HORATIO. A plastic surgeon, I believe.

PHIL. No wonder he knew so much about medicine and surgery.

HORATIO. He made women look thirty-five.

JESSICA. That's wonderful.

HORATIO. Not when they were twenty to begin with.

LINK. (*Takes newspaper clipping from envelope*) Here's a newspaper clipping on the case. With a picture of Dr. Fingers. (*Others crowd closer for a look*)

DOTTIE. That doesn't look anything like Dr. Brock.

DAVID. Give me that. (*Takes newspaper clipping, plucks pencil from a pocket, sets to work with the eraser*) I'll erase the bags under Dr. Fingers' eyes, wipe out one chin, reshape the hair style and give him a cookie duster.

MONA. The moustache makes him look like—

DAVID. You can bet on it. Dr. Fingers. Brock Rittenhouse gave himself—*a facelift!*

PHIL. Wow!

JESSICA. He was more clever than we thought!

DAVID. Looks like we can wrap this one up, Tucker.

HORATIO. What about the killer who's after me! (*Everyone has forgotten this problem. They look bewildered*)

DAVID. The important thing for now is that we've put the finger on Fingers.

HORATIO. Bah!

(*Another* FAST BLACKOUT. AD-LIB *confusion in the dark*)

LINK'S VOICE. Not again!
MONA'S VOICE. Help!
JESSICA'S VOICE. Someone ran by me in the dark!
DOTTIE'S VOICE. It's probably Dr. Brock!
DAVID'S VOICE. I got him!
PHIL'S VOICE. Don't let him get away!
LINK'S VOICE. Hold tight!
AD-LIBS.
  We've got him!
  Oh! Oh! Oh!
  Someone's stepping on my foot!

Act II   THE SOAPY MURDER CASE   49

Ouch! You're stepping on *my* foot!
Help!
(*Etc.*)

(Lights Come Up. Horatio *is in the same position he was in prior to blackout. Others are on the floor in a tight circle,* Down Center. *They don't have the killer, instead they've managed to entwine themselves in a tight ball of arms, legs, bodies as they begin to pull apart—*)

More Ad-Libs.
Careful, that's my arm.
Watch your elbow.
I think I've got someone's leg.
Easy.
(*Etc.*)
(*They manage to untangle themselves; stand*)
Mona. Where's Dr. Brock?
Horatio. You never had him, you fools. You grabbed each other in the dark. (Jessica *looks to fireplace,* Screams)
David. What is it!
Jessica. (*Points*) In the fireplace—LOOK! (*Half the group stands aside,* Left; *half* Right, *so that there's a clear unencumbered view. Dangling in the fireplace is what appears to be the below-the-knees portion of a man's body . . . white medical pants . . . white shoes and a pair of vivid red socks.* Consult Production Notes)
Phil. I'd know those red socks anywhere!
Jessica. Those white medical trousers!
Dottie. Those Pat Boone shoes!
All. BROCK RITTENHOUSE!
Horatio. (*Snarls*) You mean *Dr. Fingers*, don't you?

(Lights Fade Fast *except for a* Pin Spot *that stays focused on the legs in the fireplace, the red socks like a beacon in the dark*)

Curtain

END OF ACT TWO

ACT THREE

TIME: *Still later.*

AT RISE: HORATIO *sits in his wheelchair,* CENTER. MRS. NAUGAHIDE *is at the* UP RIGHT *table mixing medicine.* JESSICA *sits in the armchair,* MONA *on sofa,* DOTTIE *sits at table.*

HORATIO. I dislike having my library turned into a morgue. Makes things untidy.
DOTTIE. Imagine. Brock Rittenhouse—a regular Jack the Ripper.
JESSICA. I think you mean a regular Jekyll and Hyde.
DOTTIE. Them, too.
MRS. NAUGAHIDE. Obviously a split personality.
MONA. I always thought he had no personality.
LINK. (ENTERS LEFT) I don't know how much longer we can hold off the authorities.
HORATIO. We'll hold them off for as long as I say. Remember—I have your promise.
LINK. (CROSSES *to him*) There's bound to be more than a breath of scandal after two deaths.
HORATIO. The scandal no longer worries me. The identity of my unknown killer does. (MRS. NAUGAHIDE CROSSES *to* HORATIO, *holds out glass*)
MRS. NAUGAHIDE. Drink.
HORATIO. (*Distrustful*) What's in it?
MRS. NAUGAHIDE. It will settle your nerves.
HORATIO. Leave my nerves out of this.
MRS. NAUGAHIDE. Only trying to help.
HORATIO. You're always at me with a pill or something to drink. If I ever see you putting up anything with a "thumb tack" I'll know my time has come.
MRS. NAUGAHIDE. (*Angry*) I resent that, Mr. Tucker.

HORATIO. (*Motions*) Take it away, take it away. I'm not going to drink it.

MRS. NAUGAHIDE. There's a limit to my patience. (*She CROSSES back to UP RIGHT table, puts down glass. PHIL ENTERS LEFT*)

PHIL. David says no doubt about it. Dr. Brock was murdered.

JESSICA. We assumed that.

MONA. Another thumb tack attack?

PHIL. Hot lead. One of the bullets got him in his blackout. My guess is he tried to escape after he was hit.

MONA. Escape by climbing *up* the chimney? Don't be absurd.

PHIL. (*Moves to fireplace, investigates*) Maybe he was only going to hide. Wait until the coast was clear and then sneak out.

JESSICA. Or someone stuffed him up there in the blackout to hide the body.

MRS. NAUGAHIDE. It's a wonderful disguise. A face lift.

DAVID. (ENTERS LEFT) Only in Dr. Brock's case it let him down.

JESSICA. He must have plotted Ivy M. Robespierre's demise for some time. He had the confession ready.

HORATIO. (*Very puzzled*) I'm the one who's supposed to get murdered.

DAVID. One thing's as true as the nose job on Dr. Brock's false face.

HORATIO. What?

DOTTIE. I could eat something now. I didn't touch a bite at dinner.

HORATIO. Be quiet, Miss Coffee. No one's interested in your appetite. Go on, go on, Somerset.

DAVID. I mean if there's two murders already there's bound to be another. Maybe more. Murder breeds murder.

MONA. Spoken like a cynical policeman.

DAVID. (*Hard*) I know life. A cop sees a lot.

LINK. (*Takes another newspaper clipping from his pocket*) I found this in the band of Dr. Brock's jockey shorts.

JESSICA. Another clipping?

HORATIO. Give it here. (LINK *hands him the newspaper clipping.* HORATIO *pushes his spectacles to his forehead, squints*)

HORATIO. What's this? What's this? (*Squints harder*) Something about a "welfare queen." (*Squints harder still*) What's that circled in red? (*Hands clipping back*)

LINK. Her name. (*Irritated*, DAVID CROSSES *to* LINK *and grabs the clipping.* HORATIO *adjusts his glasses*)

DAVID. I'm in charge. (*Studies clipping*) Something about a "welfare queen."

LINK. (*Irritated, grabs back the clipping*) Isabelle Poe . . . seems she defrauded the state by claiming she had sixty dependent children.

MONA. They should have called her Old Mother Hubbard.

DOTTIE. Must have had her hands full with sixty kids running round the place.

MRS. NAUGAHIDE. No, No, Miss Duncan. They weren't real children.

DOTTIE. They weren't?

MRS. NAUGAHIDE. They were "imaginary" children. They didn't exist.

DOTTIE. If they didn't exist how could she have sixty of them?

HORATIO. (*Smoldering, to* LINK) Miss Dunkin' Doughnuts shouldn't be allowed to roam freely without a leash.

PHIL. Why would Dr. Brock carry that clipping around with him?

LINK. I think it's an important clue.

DAVID. (*Doubtful*) Yeah?

LINK. Look, we came here and discovered someone was out to get Mr. Tucker.

OTHERS. Right.

LINK. Only Ivy got it.

OTHERS. Right.

LINK. Who killed Ivy? Dr. Brock.

OTHERS. Right.

LINK. Who killed Dr. Brock? (*They're all about to say "Right," stop, realizing they don't know who killed him*)

DAVID. Hey! That clipping might be an important clue. (LINK *looks annoyed*) Maybe he was trying to tell us

ACT III   THE SOAPY MURDER CASE   53

that if he was murdered his killer would be old Mother Hubbard.

LINK. That's my guess—Isabelle Poe.

JESSICA. Is there a picture?

LINK. Yes. (*Hands it to* JESSICA)

JESSICA. Good heavens. Is that her face or was she storing walnuts? It's no one we know. Unless— (*Others lean toward her*) unless Dr. Fingers gave her a lift.

LINK. That's the way I have it fingered. I mean figured.

JESSICA. If we're right, one of us in this room might be —Isabelle Poe. (*Returns clipping,* LINK *pockets it*)

DAVID. Could be you, Jessica. Dottie. Mother La Mooch, or even you, Mrs. Naugahide. (*On each name, the woman* GASPS)

MONA. Unless Dr. Fingers was more skillful than anyone could have guessed. In that case, you could have killed him, David. Or you, Link. One of you could be Isabelle Poe. (*All this speculation is too much for* HORATIO. *He beats his fists on the wheelchair*)

HORATIO. Stop it, stop it. You cretins! I've never heard such applesauce! Mrs. Naugahide, fetch me that plaque. (*Indicates award plaque on mantel. She gets it, hands it to* HORATIO, *stands* RIGHT *of wheelchair*) This plaque was awarded to "The Best Tears Of Our Lives" by the Television Academy of Arts and Sciences. Each one of you was part of this award. (*Shoves it at* MRS. NAUGAHIDE) Read.

MRS. NAUGAHIDE. (*Reads*) "The Television Academy of Arts and Sciences awards this plaque to the finest half hour in daytime television, a program of quality that ranks fifth in audience appeal after the American flag, Mom, apple pie, Charlie Brown and the *Peanuts* gang."

MONA. (*Deeply touched*) That's beautiful.

JESSICA. (*Applauds softly*) I'm proud to be associated with this program. (*Others applaud politely.* MRS. NAUGAHIDE *returns plaque to mantel*)

HORATIO. THEN DO SOMETHING ABOUT THESE MURDERS! Can't you understand? Someone in this room is the killer. *It's one of you.* (*They look from one to another, horrified at the possibility*)

PHIL. (*Barely audible*) Wow. That's heavy.

HORATIO. The honor of "Tucker's Tasty Pudding Powder and All-Purpose Detergent" is at stake.

DAVID. (*Hand over his heart*) We won't fail you, sir.

DOTTIE. You know, Mr. Tucker, some people have the idea those two items are the same thing. The pudding and the detergent.

HORATIO. (*Meaningful pause*) They are the *same* thing.

DOTTIE. (*Surprised*) They are?

HORATIO. Miss Coffee—

DOTTIE. Duncan—

HORATIO. —Am I to understand you have never tasted my pudding dessert, the pudding dessert that pays your *salary?*

DOTTIE. (*She hasn't*) Well, uh, that is, uh—

HORATIO. You may serve dessert, Mrs. Naugahide.

PHIL. What are we having? (HORATIO *shoots him a withering glare.* MRS. NAUGAHIDE EXITS RIGHT)

DAVID. Brock killed Ivy, Isabelle killed Brock. Ergo, find Isabelle.

LINK. I think you have some explaining to do, Jessica.

JESSICA. (*Tenses*) I have no idea what you're talking about.

LINK. I think you do.

MONA. When you said you forgot your lines.

DOTTIE. When we did Episode Number 703.

JESSICA. I wish I could forget Episode Number 703. I'm not Isabelle Poe. This is my own face. I've had it for years. I'd no reason to murder Dr. Brock. Any one of us could be accused of murdering Ivy. We all had as much motive as Brock.

DAVID. Motive isn't always enough.

JESSICA. Come off it, David. We all wanted to get even with Ivy in some way. We all wanted to look in her attaché case. We all wanted to see the latest ratings.

DOTTIE. What became of that attaché case?

DAVID. That's right. What *did* become of it? (MRS. NAUGAHIDE ENTERS RIGHT. *She holds a tray and on the*

ACT III   THE SOAPY MURDER CASE   55

tray are small bowls of "Tucker's Tasty Pudding," spoons, one napkin)

MRS. NAUGAHIDE. Here we are. "Tucker's Tasty Pudding."

MONA. That didn't take long.

MRS. NAUGAHIDE. Only takes a second to slurp it up. Dump in the dry powder, a bit of stagnant tap water and stir.

JESSICA. (*She may be ill*) Sounds . . . delicious. (MRS. NAUGAHIDE *goes from guest to guest. They take a dish.* DIALOGUE *through blocking*)

HORATIO. Long ago I decided what's good enough for our carburetors ought to be good enough for our stomachs.

DOTTIE. (*Defensive*) I had no grudge against Ivy.

JESSICA. Don't be sly.

DOTTIE. I mean it.

JESSICA. Now who's forgotten what she said?

DOTTIE. I haven't forgotten anything.

JESSICA. In this very room, earlier, before dinner, you said—and I can recall *exactly*—"I've always wanted to poison Ivy."

DOTTIE. But I didn't. Dr. Brock did. (MRS. NAUGAHIDE *serves* HORATIO, *tucks napkin under his chin*)

HORATIO. What's this? This isn't pudding.

MRS. NAUGAHIDE. You wouldn't take your Magnetic Liver Pills, so now you can't have pudding. You know what it does to you. Makes a hard ball in your belly. (*Others spoon the mess in their bowls, hoping to whip up some enthusiasm. The conversation between* MRS. NAUGAHIDE *and* HORATIO *isn't helping*)

HORATIO. (*Petulant*) Does not make a hard ball in my belly.

MRS. NAUGAHIDE. Last time you ate some you got the hives. You stayed awake all night scratching. (SOUND *of spoons rattling in the bowls. Still, no one eats*)

HORATIO. (*Demands*) What's in this bowl?

MRS. NAUGAHIDE. Chicken soup.

HORATIO. (*He tastes*) It's heavy on the celery. (*To others*) Go on, go on. Enjoy. (*They look to one another hoping for some escape. No one wants to eat the slop.*

Finally, all at the same moment, they spoon a mouthful of the pudding, force themselves to swallow. Each tries hard not to make a distasteful face or sound. This is not possible. They all look as if they've just been poisoned)

HORATIO. Good for what ails you, right?

OTHERS. (*Smiling through their grief*)
   Right.
   Tasty.
   Wonderful flavor.
   Excellent.
   Wish I had the recipe.
   (*Etc.*)

HORATIO. Spoon it up. Does my heart good to see it. (*He tastes some more soup. Hands bowl back to* MRS. NAUGAHIDE. *She puts the tray and bowl on* UP LEFT *table. Others force themselves to eat more pudding, pained smiles on their faces. As they "enjoy,"* HORATIO *gags. His hands go to his throat. No one notices. He slips lower and lower in the wheelchair, until, with a dying moan, he falls out of chair, on the floor.* MRS. NAUGAHIDE *sees him, screams*)

MRS. NAUGAHIDE. Mr. Tucker! On the carpet! (*Others turn quickly, put down their bowls, rush to the dead man*)

MONA. Another thumb tack attack!

DAVID. (*Down on one knee, investigates*) He may still be alive.

MRS. NAUGAHIDE. I'm going to call the fire department! The paramedics! The police!

LINK. No!

MONA. If only Dr. Brock were here. He'd know what to do.

DAVID. It's too late for the fire department, the paramedics, the police or the late Dr. Brock.

DOTTIE. You mean—

DAVID. (*Great seriousness*) Horatio Tucker just slipped into the dead letter office. (*All gasp*)

PHIL. I should have worn a black tie.

LINK. Can you tell how he died?

DAVID. (*Investigates*) No marks. My guess would be— *poison. Like ivy.*

ACT III   THE SOAPY MURDER CASE   57

DOTTIE. How could it be poison? He didn't eat any of the pudding.

JESSICA. (*Goes into an emotional outburst*) Murder after murder! I'm going to crack! I'm a sensitive woman!

DAVID. Get her out of here. The body's upsetting her. (MONA *and* DOTTIE *help the distraught* JESSICA *out,* RIGHT. *In the confusion,* MRS. NAUGAHIDE *sneaks out,* LEFT)

MONA. A breath of air on the garden terrace will do you good.

JESSICA. Yes, yes. Fresh, clean air. (*They're gone.* LINK, DAVID *and* PHIL *stare down at the body*)

PHIL. What do you think we ought to do?

LINK. Find Isabelle Poe before she kills us all.

PHIL. (*Points to body*) What about Old Dan Tucker? (*Corrects himself*) I mean old *man* Tucker.

DAVID. He's a closed book. We'll put him in the library.

LINK. One of us ought to keep an eye on the women. Don't forget one of them has to be Isabelle.

PHIL. I'll go.

(PHIL EXITS RIGHT. NOTE: *Now begins a routine of comic stage shtick as* DAVID *and* LINK *attempt to move the body.* HORATIO *has slid from his wheelchair to the floor and landed on his back*)

DAVID. I'll take his feet. You take his head. (*They position the body so its feet face* DAVID, *its head faces* LINK. DAVID *picks up the feet easily.* LINK *lifts the head, but this is clumsy and he can't hold on*)

LINK. Won't work. Drop it. (*They drop the body*)

DAVID. Take his arms. (LINK *takes the arms, pulling them back over the dead man's head.* DAVID *grabs the ankles*) When I say "lift," lift.

LINK. Gotcha.

DAVID. Lift. (*They lift the body, only* HORATIO *sags so that his bottom drags on the floor as they take a few steps* LEFT)

LINK. No good.

DAVID. Drop it. (*They drop the body*) Turn him over. (*They turn* HORATIO *over so that he's face down*)
LINK. Now what?
DAVID. I'll take his head. You take his feet. (*They do a reversal of the first attempt*)
LINK. Say "lift."
DAVID. Lift. (*They lift.* DAVID *has trouble with his end*) No good, either. (*They drop the body*)
LINK. Take his arms. (DAVID *pulls* HORATIO'S *arms over his head.* LINK *grabs the ankles*) Say "lift."
DAVID. Lift. (*They lift the body, only now it's* HORATIO'S *belly that drags the floor as they attempt to carry him out*)
LINK. Still no good. (*They drop the body.* HORATIO *is stretched out, face down, on the floor*)
DAVID. I know. (*He steps behind the corpse, reaches down and grabs hold of* HORATIO'S *belt, or his robe, and slowly pulls upwards so that* HORATIO *is gradually lifted by the back mid-section. His hands and feet remain on the floor. He looks as if he were practicing some Yoga position*)
LINK. We can't leave him like that! Looks like a pretzel.
DAVID. Get the chair.
LINK. What chair?
DAVID. The wheelchair. (LINK *gets it*) Put it behind him. (LINK *positions the wheelchair behind* HORATIO, *who remains in that ridiculous position.* DAVID *acts like a traffic cop, motioning with his hands*) Okay. Move it in. Move it close. Easy does it. (*Inch by inch,* LINK *moves the seat of the chair closer and closer to* HORATIO'S *rump, until the seat is touching the back of the dead man's legs*) Hold that wheelchair steady.
LINK. Gotcha. (DAVID *stands in front of* HORATIO. *He puts his middle finger against the dead's man's forehead and slowly applies pressure, carefully "lifting" the corpse until its hands are off the floor.* HORATIO *is now in a "half-standing," ape-like position.* DAVID *keeps his finger on the forehead, using steady pressure*)
DAVID. Push in the chair. Easy. Easy. (LINK *eases the wheelchair under* HORATIO, *so that when* DAVID *gives a*

slight shove with his finger, the body falls upward and backward and lands upright in the seat. Horatio's *arms dangle lifelessly, his head to one side*) Exit the body. (*They push the latest victim out*, LEFT)

Mona's Voice. (*From* Off Right) I've never seen Jessica behave that way.

Dottie's Voice. (*From* Off Right) She was really upset. (*They* Enter)

Mona. Small wonder.

Dottie. I think the pudding might have had something to do with it. That would scare anyone.

Mona. (*Looks at spot where* Horatio *died*) The body's gone, thankfully. (Dottie Crosses *to the sofa, sits.* Mona *stands by table*)

Dottie. That pudding tasted like butterscotch dust.

Mrs. Naugahide's Voice. (*From* Off Left) Let me go! Take your hands off me! I'm no criminal!

David's Voice. (*From* Off Left) I should have suspected you'd be up to something.

Dottie. What's that?

Mona. It's Mrs. Naugahide. (David Enters *with a struggling* Mrs. Naugahide)

Mrs. Naugahide. I'll have your badge for this.

David. We've got the honor of the show at stake.

Mrs. Naugahide. I pay your salary! I'm a taxpayer! (David *pushes her into the armchair, takes out a pair of handcuffs, pulls her arms behind the back of the chair, cuffs her.* Dottie *jumps to her feet, alarmed*)

Dottie. What are you doing?

David. I'm not playing checkers.

Mona. What's she done?

David. We found her in the hallway—*on the phone.* She was dialing the police.

Mona. (*Disappointed*) Oh, Mrs. Naugahide. We all agreed. No police.

Mrs. Naugahide. I never made such a promise. Uncuff me, Officer Somerset.

David. No way.

Mrs. Naugahide. I always thought you were such a nice, friendly neighborhood policeman.

David. (*Tough*) Murder changes us all.

Mrs. Naugahide. I'll scream and scream and scream.
David. Mona, quick, an apple.
Mona. This is no time to think of food.
David. Hurry! (Mona *gets an apple from the bowl on* Up Right *table*)
Mrs. Naugahide. You've got no right to keep me here. I don't want to be murdered.
David. Behave and there won't be any trouble.
Mrs. Naugahide. *Help!*
David. Quiet!
Mrs. Naugahide. *Help, help!*
David. You asked for it. (Mona *tosses the apple to* Dottie *who tosses it to* David)
Mrs. Naugahide. *Help! Help! Help!* (*Using the apple for a gag,* David *sticks it in* Mrs. Naugahide's *mouth. Her eyes bulge in outrage*)
David. That'll hold her.
Link. (Enters Left, *moves* Left *of* Mrs. Naugahide) Telephoning is a no-no, Mrs. Naugahide. I know it's not easy, but we've got to stick it out.
David. (*Moves to* Center) Want to tell us about it, Dottie?
Dottie. (*Tenses*) I don't know what you're talking about.
Link. Earlier this evening Dr. Brock said he didn't know what he was going to do if the show was cancelled.
Mona. (*Remembers*) And you said—
Dottie. (*Resigned*) I said—"There are always jobs for a doctor or a surgeon."
Mona. Dr. Brock was furious when you said that. You *knew* who he was.
Dottie. (*Sits dejectedly on sofa*) Yes, I knew who he was. He knew who I was. We both knew who we were. (*Touches her face*) I got a lift from Fingers.
Mona. You're Isabelle Poe.
Dottie. I *was* Isabelle Poe. I was paying everything back. Ten dollars a month, plus interest and late payment charges. I'll tell you something else— (Jessica *stands in entryway,* Right) He got more fan mail than anyone else because I had to write it! Night after night

writing fan mail to the man who was blackmailing me.
  DAVID. You could have exposed him.
  DOTTIE. I would have lost my job. That was more important to me than anything. "Tears" restored my character, although I admit it wasn't much to begin with.
  MONA. "Tears"?
  DOTTIE. No, my character. If I didn't keep my job on the soap how else would I be able to pay the money back? (*Dramatic*) Dr. Brock Rittenhouse, A.K.A. Dr. Fingers, was—no good.
  JESSICA. (ENTERS, *steps* DOWN RIGHT) You're right, Dottie. If they gave out medals for being a rotter he would have been weighted down with tin and ribbon. I even saw Ivy M. Robespierre in his arms.
  OTHERS. Yeech.
  JESSICA. (*Chokes back a sob*) He borrowed money and costume jewelry from me. Gambled it away. Under his hospital whites and dirty red socks beat the heart of a no-goody-two-shoes. (*Sits at table.* PHIL *appears at entryway,* LEFT) When I told him I loved him—he laughed.
  MONA. The beast.
  JESSICA. (*Imitates* DR. BROCK's *cruel laugh*) "Ha" he said. "Ha, ha, ha." Then, he said it again. "Ha, ha, ha." (*Melodramatic*) I'm so weak.
  MRS. NAUGAHIDE. (*Mumbling with apple in her mouth*) Ugh, mmm, auuuuugh, oooow . . .
  JESSICA. Easy enough for you to say that, Mrs. Naugalint—Naugadyed—Naugahide—whatever your name is, but you forget— (*Soap oper-ish feeling*) I was a— "prisoner of love."
  DAVID. (*Like a facilitator in a therapy session*) That was intimate, Jessica. Thanks for sharing it with the group. (*Looks about*) Anyone else?
  LINK. I think we're getting closer and closer to the truth.
  MONA. Are we?
  LINK. Aren't we?
  MONA. Ivy M. Robespierre mentioned that she had a copy of the script in her attaché case. The attaché case is missing, yet you had a script when we did Episode Number 703.

DOTTIE. That's right!

LINK. I always carry the latest script around with me. You all know that.

DOTTIE. Do we?

JESSICA. I happen to know Ivy was planning to direct the show herself. You had an excellent motive to get her out of the way.

LINK. You forget—Brock killed Ivy.

JESSICA. (*Thinks*) That's right. I did forget.

DAVID. Wait a minute. How come we didn't die after we ate the pudding?

PHIL. Because Mr. Tucker had chicken soup. (*Looks to* MRS. NAUGAHIDE) Heavy on the celery. (MRS. NAUGAHIDE *shakes her head from side to side, denying any guilt, the apple still in her mouth*)

DOTTIE. (*Points to* MONA) Mother La Mooch brought the soup.

MONA. Don't try to spill the grease on me.

DOTTIE. Shouldn't someone notify Mr. Tucker's family? It would be polite.

LINK. Good idea. Ask Mrs. Naugahide. (DAVID *steps to her, removes apple*)

MRS. NAUGAHIDE. (*Angrily*) No sense asking me. I've only worked for that disagreeable gentleman for a few days.

OTHERS. What!

MRS. NAUGAHIDE. I've only been here since Monday.

JESSICA. You've only been acquainted with him for a few days?

MRS. NAUGAHIDE. Seems like a lifetime.

LINK. Wait a minute, wait a minute. The clue in Episode Number 703.

PHIL. There wasn't any.

LINK. Exactly. Don't you see? That whole business of a clue in the script was a phony dodge of some kind. (HORATIO *has wheeled himself to the entryway*, LEFT, *blanket over his legs*)

HORATIO. You're smarter than I gave you credit for, Kennecott. (*Everyone is astonished*)

PHIL. You're alive!

HORATIO. Officer Somerset, be kind enough to push me

in. (DAVID *hesitates*) I'm not dead, you coconut. (DAVID *still doesn't move.* HORATIO *takes out a revolver*) I said—push me in. (DAVID *swallows hard, pushes* HORATIO *to in front of fireplace. Others are in a state of shock*) Don't stand behind me, Somerset. (*Motions with revolver*) Get where I can see you. (DAVID *steps* LEFT *of wheelchair*)

LINK. Mr. Tucker, why are you doing all this?
HORATIO. I'm not Tucker. Don't you recognize me?
LINK. No.
HORATIO. Don't any of you recognize me? (*They shake their heads*) Maybe you'll recall the names of Cecily Moonstone and Lottie Crummond.
DOTTIE. Written out of the show.
HORATIO. Careers ruined by Ivy M. Robespierre. They took it gracefully: used Avon products and garage sales, but I vowed I'd get even. (*He tosses aside the blanket, stands. Removes spectacles, pulls off bushy eyebrows. Others freeze into an exaggerated tableau of astonishment*)
LINK. It's you!
OTHERS.
 Amazing.
 I never would have believed it.
 Incredible.
 Impossible.
 (*Etc.*)
MRS. NAUGAHIDE. Astonishing. (*Pause*) Who is he?
MONA. Lionel Shumway.
MRS. NAUGAHIDE. Who?

(NOTE: *The humor of the "revelation" lies in the fact there is almost no difference in appearance between* LIONEL SHUMWAY *and his impersonation of* HORATIO TUCKER. *The invalid pose, the spectacles, the bushy eyebrows—so much for the "disguise"*)

LINK. Last time I saw you you were down in Chinatown, by the Bowery, bumming spare change.
HORATIO/LIONEL. I saved every penny I bummed to rent this penthouse. I knew none of you had ever seen the real Tucker. I knew none of you would refuse his invitation. I practiced my impersonation on Mrs. Imitation Leather.

MRS. NAUGAHIDE. Could have fooled me.
HORATIO/LIONEL. I *did* fool you, you fool.
MRS. NAUGAHIDE. I was a fool to be taken in like that.
DOTTIE. You killed Ivy.
HORATIO/LIONEL. I *punished* Ivy. I knew who Brock was. I planned to put the blame on him. After that I wanted people to think you did it, Dottie. I knew you were Isabelle Poe.
DOTTIE. What a cruel thing to do to an actress.
HORATIO/LIONEL. You're not an actress. You're an alias.
JESSICA. You wanted to *ruin* the soap. *Revenge.*
HORATIO/LIONEL. That was the original plan. But when I saw you all again, I thought, why should you have everything and I have nothing?
MRS. NAUGAHIDE. You have this lovely apartment.
HORATIO/LIONEL. (*Rage building*) I was a better actor than any of you. I never got the applause I deserved.
DAVID. He's not playing with a full deck.
LINK. He's out to lunch.
DOTTIE. It's cuckoo time in mid-Manhattan.
HORATIO/LIONEL. *Shut up!*
DAVID/LINK/DOTTIE. (*Meekly*) Sorry.
PHIL. Play fair, Lionel. When you were on the soap there was only one thing lower than our ratings—the pits.
MONA. The lower depths.
JESSICA. The absolute bottom. (HORATIO/LIONEL *growls in rage*)
MRS. NAUGAHIDE. Careful. Looks like he's going to bite.
DAVID. How many bullets in that revolver?
HORATIO/LIONEL. Six.
MRS. NAUGAHIDE. There are seven of us.
HORATIO/LIONEL. I reload fast.
MONA. You mean you're actually going to do this because you're jealous! You're going to play dog-in-the-manger?
HORATIO/LIONEL. If I can't be part of "The Best Tears Of Our Lives" no one can. (*Prepares to fire*) I'm turning this place into a shooting gallery. (DOTTIE, MONA, MRS. NAUGAHIDE *scream*)
PHIL. Somebody do something!

ACT III THE SOAPY MURDER CASE 65

JESSICA. (*Thinking fast*) You were wonderful in your impersonation of Horatio Tucker, Lionel. Brilliant! Superb! I never would have believed it. What a talent!

HORATIO/LIONEL. (*Pleased*) How's that again? (JESSICA *applauds*)

JESSICA. An incredible performance. You ought to get a Tony Award. (JESSICA's *ploy is beginning to work.* HORATIO/LIONEL *is lapping up the compliments, begins to smile*)

HORATIO/LIONEL. Tony Award?

DOTTIE. Tony Award, nothing. An *Academy* Award. (*Applauds*) Encore! Encore!

HORATIO/LIONEL. Academy Award?

LINK. Best Actor of the Century Award!

HORATIO/LIONEL. (*Bedazzled*) Best Actor of the Century? (LINK *applauds. Soon everyone, except* MRS. NAUGAHIDE, *whose hands are still cuffed, is applauding wildly*)

AD-LIBS.
  Bravo! Bravo!
  Author! Author!
  Brilliant performance, brilliant!

PHIL. Give him the Nobel Prize! Give him the Pulitzer Prize! (*Whistles, stomping of feet, etc.* HORATIO/LIONEL *responds happily to the ovation.* MONA *runs* OFFSTAGE, *scoops up the floral arrangement in the hallway, runs back and presents the "bouquet" to* HORATIO/LIONEL. *Completely forgetting reality, he passes the revolver to* DAVID *so his arms are free to accept the flowers. The applause trickles off . . .* HORATIO/LIONEL *continues to bow, muttering* "Thank you, too kind. Too kind." *He stops, a horror-stricken expression on his face as he realizes he's been had*)

DAVID. (*Motions with revolver*) Come on, Lionel. You've got a date at the station house.

HORATIO/LIONEL. (*Shrugs*) What do I care! I've just given the performance of my life. You heard what they said. They loved me. I was brilliant. (*Like a great stage tragedian, the flowers pressed to his chest as tribute,* HORATIO/LIONEL CROSSES LEFT *turns, strikes a theatrical pose at the entryway*) I al ys knew I was too good for soap opera. I should have ...ed Shakespeare! ɪ wouldn't have been *merely* brilliant. I would have been— (*One arm up for emphasis*) *fabulous!* (*He* Exits)

Phil. What a ham.

David. He's due for padded wallpaper.

Phil. The only award he's going to get is the booby prize.

Mrs. Naugahide. Will somebody *please* get me out of these handcuffs!

David. Take care of it, Phil. I'll see to Shumway. (Phil *steps in;* David *gives him some keys.* David Exits Left. Phil *steps to armchair, removes cuffs.* Dialogue Through)

Mona. Now I know why this apartment looked familiar. It *is* the same one we use on the soap.

Link. A copy. Shumway was mad, but clever. (Mrs. Naugahide *is freed, stands*)

Mrs. Naugahide. I'll have my hat on my head and be out the door before you can say "Tucker's Tasty Pudding Powder And All-Purpose Detergent." (*She hurries Off, Right*)

Link. I better call the public relations department at the network. They'll want to know about this. (*He Exits, Left*)

Mona. I'm heading for the nearest subway.

Phil. I'll go with you.

Mona. Why?

Phil. There are muggers out there. A person could get hurt.

Mona. Thank you, Phil. You're thoughtful.

Phil. Safety in numbers. (Mona *and* Phil Exit)

Dottie. A person could get hurt out there! What about in here?

Jessica. What an experience.

Dottie. I don't care what anyone says about life in suburbia. I'll be glad to get back to pleasant Pine Valley.

Jessica. I know what you mean. New York's fun to visit. But I wouldn't want to live here. (*They move to Exit*)

Fast Curtain

END OF PLAY

PRODUCTION NOTES

PROPERTIES:
Act One—(On Stage): Table with 2 chairs, narrow tables or sideboards (2) with decanters, bric-a-brac, glasses, etc., bowl of apples on UP RIGHT table, fireplace with mantel, framed award or plaque, sofa, large armchair, sidetable, floral arrangement on small table in hallway (OFF RIGHT) additional chairs (2), portrait of HORATIO as young man. Add stage dressing as desired: carpets, lamps, wall hangings, lamps, et al.

(Brought On): Shawl, blanket, handkerchief, spectacles (HORATIO, prior to curtain); tray with medicine and tablespoon (prior to curtain). Walking stick or cane (MRS. NAUGAHIDE); attaché case with papers, folders, script (IVY); apron and wheelchair (MRS. NAUGAHIDE); medical bag (DR. BROCK); folded letter (HORATIO); flower (IVY, plucked from floral arrangement in hallway); bamboo pole being pushed through portrait's mouth by someone unseen; dinner gong and hammer (MRS. NAUGAHIDE).

Act Two—(Brought On): Surgical mask and gloves, (DR. BROCK); policeman's jacket and hat, key, pencil with eraser (DAVID); wheelchair (HORATIO); script (LINK); dagger or knife with envelope and newspaper clipping, confession letter (stuck into armchair during first blackout); hat pin (MONA).

Act Three—(Brought On): Wheelchair (HORATIO); a second newspaper clipping (LINK); tray with bowls (7) of pudding, one bowl supposedly holds chicken soup, one napkin (MRS. NAUGAHIDE); handcuffs (DAVID); blanket and revolver (HORATIO).

PRODUCTION NOTES

SOUND EFFECTS:
Doorbell, organ music, pistol shots (3). (Blanks can be fired OFFSTAGE during first blackout by crew person.)

LIGHTING:
General stage lighting; blackout (2); lighting to suggest television studio for taping of soap opera; pinspot or special light to focus on red socks in fireplace.

COSTUMES:
Modern summer clothing. Indicated here are only those that are specifically mentioned in the text for some plot or character purpose: dark dress with starched white apron and maid's cap (MRS. NAUGAHIDE); fashionable but severe outfit (IVY); glamorous outfit (JESSICA); thin cloth coat with ratty fur collar and hat (MONA); sweater, bow tie, glasses (PHIL); HORATIO might wear pajamas, robe and slippers.

GENERAL NOTES:
Lower portion of Dr. Brock's body in fireplace: Depending on how the fireplace is constructed, actor playing role might be able to lower himself into view from behind—the important thing is that the feet "dangle" since the victim has been pushed up the chimney and is, supposedly, slipping down. If this isn't feasible, simply have the lower part of a pair of white pants, red socks and white shoes (stuffed to suggest Dr. Brock's body) tucked up in the fireplace, out of audience view. When the second blackout occurs, performer closest to the fireplace reaches up and pulls the "feet" down.

Link and David move Horatio's body: This is always a great audience pleaser as two men attempt to move an uncooperative corpse. During this wild nonsense, director may come up with even more outrageous business to add. If it works, and it's funny, use it.

OTHER TITLES AVAILABLE FROM BAKER'S PLAYS

THE COOLEY GIRLS

Brad Stephens

Dramatic Comedy / 1m, 5f

Three sisters, Rose, Brenda and Harriet Cooley, have been separated since childhood. Now forty years later, one of the sisters, Rose, decides to find her lost siblings and reunite the 'girls'. All of them have secrets to hide, but it is curiosity that finally brings them together for their unexpected reunion. Only when Harriet is forced to admit her most damning secret does this hard-bitten and humorous play resolve once and for all the bond each shares with the other. Perfect for community stages.

BAKERSPLAYS.COM

OTHER TITLES AVAILABLE FROM BAKER'S PLAYS

SEE YOU IN BELLS

Edie Claire

Comedy / 6m, 6f, 2 teen girls, 1 teen boy, and a good-natured minister / A church sanctuary

The mother of the bride has every reason to panic. Three generations of Bower family weddings—three inexplicable disasters. Now, with the church building falling down, half the wedding party AWOL, and the bride's sisters still fighting over what happened at the last family wedding, daughter Jenna's nuptials seem hopelessly doomed. But peacemaking brother Brian is determined to end the sisters' feud—and the family curse. All he needs is to stage a rip-roaring intervention…and pray it turns divine!

OTHER TITLES AVAILABLE FROM BAKER'S PLAYS

KEEPSAKES

Pat Cook

Drama / 4m, 6f / Interior

Ever look at a family portrait and wonder what those people, posed and smiling, are really like? This family portrait shows you the inner workings of the Rogers family – how they deal with everyday things, how they deal with both happy and sad events which effect each and every one of them. These funny, poignant and all-too-human characters go through life the best way they know how.

Austin does his best to keep the house running smoothly, unless he has to take Pawpaw's trunk out of the basement. Mary Jo is outwardly pleased when son Mitchell gets engaged to Tish but explains "They're too young!" Her sister, Brenda, helps out by saying "Not any younger than you were when you got married." Brenda's husband, Dale, has his own advice for young Mitchell – "Marriage consists in large part of just giving up!" And Pawpaw keeps hearing voices and seeing people who aren't there.

The very fabric of the family unit meets its ultimate challenge when Brenda and Dale have to move in with them. Daughter Jan has to put up with a whiney dog, Mitchell and Tish can't seem to find time to talk about their upcoming marriage and everyone is bunking up with everyone else, leaving the men to sleep on the couch – any of this sound familiar? Brought to you by the same author of *Good Help is So Hard to Murder*.

BAKERSPLAYS.COM

www.ingramcontent.com/pod-product-compliance
Lightning Source LLC
Chambersburg PA
CBHW071841290426
44109CB00017B/1896